Anne is a walking mirc
challenge and enco
I wholeheartedly com.
as a person who prophetically lives out and
'soars like an eagle' as she teaches faith.
Rev Rob Cotton, Author of Hope in the Main Street

An inspirational life journey of spiritual growth and
affirmation of faith. The descriptions of healing in
response to serious illness are strong,
positive and enabling.
Andrew Amos, Consultant Haematologist,
Staffordshire, UK

In her masterpiece, Anne highlights her faith journey
with a faithful God whose love surpasses all things.
The divine encounter with the Holy Spirit changed
Anne's life trajectory and God continues to use her
in uncountable ways across the globe as a source
of encouragement for all to embrace their
identity in Christ.
Rose Mugabi Khalayi, Women Ministry Director of
Pastors Discipleship Network, Uganda, and
Co-founder of Lily Olympia Africa

Come along with Anne on her journey with El Shaddai,
God Almighty, step by step, from glory to glory, into
the reality of the miraculous!
Rev David Lebo, Author of Abiding Under The Shadow
and Founder of Tidal Wave Ministries Int.,
West Virginia, USA

You will finish this book with the desire to read more from Anne. This story highlights important aspects of New Testament faith-living. Anne's writing will show you how, and inspire you to discover your identity as a child of God.

**Pastor John and Sandra Tyrell,
Community Life Church, Cannock, UK**

I know that it will be a great blessing for your life to know that if God the Almighty transformed Anne's life, He will also do it in yours, because His love for you is infinite. Enjoy reading!

**Luis Alberto Pequeño Chávez,
Red Kairos Ministry, Peru**

As you read this book, may you meet Jesus in its pages. May you catch Anne's zest for life, and may you too be captivated by God's far greater story of bringing life in all its fullness.

**Rev Andy and Tina Woof,
Garstang Free Methodist Church,
Lancashire, UK**

Anne's life journey, experiences, struggles, life's pains and joys, her growing faith, gained trust and dependence upon her Lord Jesus is extremely relatable and contagiously desirable. This book is truly a blessing from our Lord Jesus to guide and help you in being His workmanship, created in Christ Jesus for good works, which God has ordained, that we should walk in Him.

**Pastor Mark Blankenbeckler,
Glory City Church Network, USA**

GOD
SPLIT
THE
SEA

Thank you for being
part of my story.

love you,

Anne x

Issachar Global Publishing
PO Box 38082
London
SW19 1YQ
UK
www.issacharglobal.com

Thank you

To various close friends who have supported and encouraged me, as well as assisting in so many ways to get the book ready for publication. Especially Alan, for the constancy and faithfulness of your love and support. Your steady, solid trust that what God has spoken will be, not only releases, but launches me to fulfil God's call.

To our children, Philip and Emma, Charlotte and Austin, and our grandchildren, Grace, Thomas, Lydia, William and Keziah for being such an integral part of our lives and ongoing story. The joy of sharing faith with you all is beyond expression.

To Jackie Knott, for the watercolour painting featured in the cover design.

To those, too many to name, who have helped resolve grammar and sentence structure issues! You know who you are! Your selfless giving of time is so appreciated.

To God, for creating this story, inspiring this book, and placing in my life all those mentioned above, named and unnamed.

ANNE DONALDSON

Chapters

ANNE DONALDSON

Foreword

I first met Anne as a young teenager, fresh into faith and excited by all that God had to offer. In Anne, my friends and I found one of the few people we knew who believed what the Bible said and lived it out. She became to us 'Anne the Oracle' — our sounding board, the person we could turn to receive wisdom, understanding and love.

As a teenager who wanted Jesus, knowing an adult for whom what God said seemed to come far above what might be thought of as sensible, or normal or the 'right thing' allowed me, and others, to grow in freedom and a greater desire for God.

Reading Anne's book, I have been fascinated to find what similarities there were in both our backgrounds. In the tradition I was brought up in, it seemed that teaching on the Holy Spirit was somewhere between rare and non-existent. Therefore, as God began to teach me and fill me with His presence, Anne became a teacher and leader, a pioneer in the things of God who I would love to follow, if only I could keep up! Little did I know at that stage that years later I would fall in love with, and end up marrying her daughter!

Anne has fulfilled many roles throughout my life: youth leader; teacher; discipler; mentor; mother-in-law and, of course, friend. Throughout approximately 30 years, she has followed Christ in such a way that it continually challenges and encourages me to aspire to a walk in a relationship like hers.

There are not many Christian leaders I know who could authentically say as Paul does,

> *"Imitate me, just as I also imitate Christ."*
> **1 Corinthians 11:1**

But Anne can definitely be counted as one of them.

It is from her foundation of faith and relationship with Jesus that Anne has lived out her life with Jesus, no matter what the enemy has thrown at her. As I have thought over many of the trials that Anne has been subjected to since I have known her, there are a couple of verses in scripture which I have felt apply to her life.

The first is spoken by Joseph in Genesis 50. Speaking to his father and to his brothers, who had sold him into slavery, he says,

> *"You meant evil against me; but God meant it for good, in order to bring it about as it is this day, to save many people."*
> **Genesis 50:20**

Anne's partnership with God as she battled cancer and took victory over the illness is something which the enemy meant for evil. He meant to destroy her and our family and damage the faith of many who knew and loved her. But God has used it for good, and through Anne's experience and God's grace, many lives have been saved, more have strengthened their relationship with Him and I believe that through her ongoing testimony, many more will also be saved.

The second verse that I find so relevant when I think of Anne's battle with cancer is similar:

"And we know that all things work together for good to those who love God, to those who are the called according to His purpose."
Romans 8:28

It really is ALL things that God will work for our good.

We don't always see it at the time, in fact we rarely do, but God does not waste any circumstance of life. I have seen it in my life, and with my own health struggles. But in Anne the truth of this is plain to see. I know that even for just one person to have found Christ and be saved for eternity through hearing her story Anne would tell you it was worth it. But God is a God of abundance and He will save and impact many as He makes everything work together for good to those who love Him.

Reading this book has, for me, added to the already phenomenal respect and love I have for Anne and Alan. I have been reminded of things and discovered situations I wasn't fully aware of. In every situation as a couple they mirror the glory and love of God as they trust and follow Him.

RT Kendall, in his excellent book on Hebrews 11, describes faith as 'believing God'. Not just believing in God, but believing Him in all things. That everything He says is trustworthy and true and when He says something will happen, it will occur. Anne's account of her illness, healing, recovery and walk with God will allow you to watch her believing God in every aspect of her life. It will enlarge your faith in the God who is worth believing.

Austin Foote
November 2021

If this is true, then this is the most dynamic, most exciting, most amazing thing in the whole wide world.

Chapter One
The Background

"I can confidently say that you have cancer, but what this biopsy will tell us is what sort of cancer." The consultant smiled as she answered the question that I had just posed: "Do you think that this might be cancer?"

It was the Monday at the start of Holy Week in 2001. The conversation between myself and the consultant followed on from a consultation in 1999 when I first noticed some very small bumps appearing on my scalp. I had been referred to the consultant by my GP after enquiring about what they might be. At that first consultation, a biopsy was taken from one of these at the nape of my head. When I returned three weeks later for the results, I was told that the histology was hard to read.

I was reassured, however, that it was nothing at all to be concerned about and that the best thing to do was to go away and forget about it. That is exactly what I did. I just thought that they would eventually go away and I got on with life.

Let me take you back to the very beginning: I was born and brought up in a Christian home and taken to church every Sunday – twice with Sunday school! I liked the people there and had good friendships, but I found the services dull and irrelevant. I loved the singing; I have always loved singing!

My parents were farmers and the countryside where we lived was beautiful. It was wonderful to roam the fields, play in the streams, walk amongst the wild flowers, climb trees, make dens, help on the farm calving, feeding the hens, chicks, ducks and lambs. My childhood was very protected in that we only went to church on Sundays and the cattle market on Wednesdays, so I tended to mix with a small group of family and friends and the same applied to our social life.

From an early age, I perceived a sadness which I associated with my birthday each year. Growing up, I learnt that my maternal grandmother had died shortly before my birth and that my mother had gone into labour as she left the graveside. Mum always speaks of what a joy and blessing my birth was to her and how that helped her through her grief. My childhood perception marred my birthdays but God would one day deal with this in an awesome way.

Apparently, I was a determined little one, as can be seen by the story told of me when my sister, Ruth, three years older than me, had problems with a certain boy at the village primary school. It was my plan to "get him" as soon as I was old enough to join her at school. And get him I did!

Teddy, who went everywhere with me, was used as a weapon. Holding the bear's legs, and using the rest of his body, I beat this poor child. This did resolve the problem for Ruth, and also established something that still exists today: the deepest bond between us. We really look out for one another, though not with physical weapons now!

(As for Teddy, I still have him, though I no longer carry him around.)

As a young girl, I would be chatty and outgoing in the company of those I knew well, but was otherwise very shy. Also, I hated anything that took me by surprise. Two examples from my young days fell quite close together within the calendar year: the dreaded Sunday School Anniversary and the Staffordshire County Show.

The show should have been a happy day — in fact, I really wanted to go and would, in those days, be allowed time off school so that we could go as a family. Meeting other relatives, we would chat and laugh, engaging in the farming life that I so loved. A display team in the main ring would, however, fire explosives creating unexpected loud booms and bangs that froze me with terror. The unexpected unsettled me and that carried through a lot of my life. Each spring, I also anticipated the horror of standing high up on a specially erected stage in the front of the church. Despite practising songs and recitations for weeks beforehand, when the day arrived I would literally freeze with nerves and cry. There were strangers sitting in the pews and I wasn't used to that. The memories of this are still so vivid. I was terrified of being asked to perform. Family and friends even resorted to bribing me with a 'thruppence' or sweets, but to no avail.

Even as I grew, when asked to do anything in church I literally struggled to stand due to shaking legs and trembling hands. But the majority of the time I found church so boring that I never really looked forward to Sundays, apart from when we had company after the evening service.

My mother would play from the old hymnals and I loved the really jolly lively choruses. My favourites were from the old Sankey and Moody Hymnal, although I didn't know back then their words carried such truth and foundational teaching. At times, during Sunday services, I would really want to respond to what I was hearing but didn't know what I needed to do to become a Christian. I knew that I needed to make some sort of response as there were people around me who had a different sort of relationship with God than I did. There was one elderly gentleman in our church family who was more than a church attendee. He appeared to have such a direct link with God that when he prayed I used to move physically closer to him because I imagined some sort of invisible shaft going from him direct to God. I thought if I sat near this gentleman then God would see me too.

I particularly remember when I was about seven or eight years old my mother playing an old hymn called 'Near the Cross'.

"Jesus keep me near the cross; there a precious fountain. Free to all, a healing stream flows from Calvary's mountain. In the cross, in the cross, be my glory ever, 'til my raptured soul shall find rest beyond the river."

I remember starting to cry and not understanding why! Somehow, I just knew that what I was singing was something far bigger than me and I sensed a strange presence that was so beautiful that it touched me deep inside. Looking back now, I realise that this was the Holy Spirit at work.

When I was nine years old, we had a wonderful addition to our family: my brother Michael. As with Ruth, I utterly loved him and wanted to protect him. The three of us are so thankful to have such a bond of love and to have shared such a lovely childhood. Ruth, Michael and I had fun playing with the animals, and one another. Ruth and I, being closer in age, did get up to all sorts of pranks!

One small area of the farm was a disused gravel pit. We used to take Michael in his pushchair to have an adventure there. One of us dragged him up to the top of the bank in the buggy and let it go careering down, whilst the other stood at the bottom to catch.

I was a carefree youngster, enjoying life, until a couple of incidents rocked my world. Both took place as I was entering my teenage years.

The first was when an older boy sexually assaulted me as I walked through the countryside on an errand for my parents. This incident made me aware of a world I hadn't known existed. Those I tried to confide in didn't take it seriously and I lived in fear of him doing it again until his family left the area. I felt wronged but thought it didn't matter to anyone so I bottled up my feelings. I don't blame anyone for not listening because at that time young people were not listened to in the way that they are today. But in my later teens further incidents to myself and others close to me compounded a deeper fear and damaged my identity as a female.

My view of sexuality affected my attitude towards men. Years later, when experiencing the purity of God's love, I was set free and healed.

The second incident was the death of my grandfather. I hadn't been exposed to bereavement before and the shock was multi-faceted. I had never seen my father express such emotion and these natural expressions of grief shook me but were not spoken about. It was agreed, between my parents, that instead of attending the funeral I would look after Michael and I didn't have the opportunity to express my desire to go. When we joined the tea afterwards, I was breaking inside but arrived to find people laughing, talking, and enjoying refreshments. I was so angry. It's my first memory of feeling such a depth of anger. How dare they enjoy themselves as though nothing had happened? I wanted to shout and tell them all to go home. Again, I held all this inside, although I was sent home from school on a number of occasions during the followings weeks because I was crying unconsolably. The tears were an expression of what was going on inside me that I felt unable to express verbally; my feelings and desires were of little or no value. I felt I was neither understood nor listened to. This continued for decades.

Even as a mature adult, when I was perceived as doing or saying something which was not in my heart, this misreading of my motives could cause me to sob unconsolably. It was only through understanding what God says about me, of the importance He places on the desires of our hearts and that He knows our intentions, that set me free from those lies and the hold they had on me. A wonderful truth is found in Psalm 37: 4–6 (NIV).

"Delight yourself in the LORD and he will give you the desires of your heart.

"Commit your way to the LORD; trust in him and he will do this:
he will make your righteous reward shine like the dawn, the justice of your cause like the noonday sun."

Psalm 37: 4–6 (NIV)

When I was 14, I began studying for my O Level exams. That year, the study for Religious Education was the Gospel of Luke and the Acts of the Apostles. I loved it! It was the first time that I had read the Gospel followed by the Acts of the Apostles in this way. You see, at church we would hear about 'Daniel in the Lion's Den' one week, and then 'Jesus walking on the water' the next, followed by 'Noah and The Ark' and so on. I had never realised that the various stories were actually linked.

In this educational setting, with formal study and disciplined essay writing, I saw for the very first time how they were all linked: through Jesus. The study in Luke's Gospel began with the statements about the coming baby fulfilling prophecy, leading on to the birth of Jesus, His life and ministry; His journey to the cross, death, resurrection, the empty tomb, appearing to the disciples, His ascension, the outpouring of His Spirit at Pentecost, as promised, and the start and growth of the early church. It was brilliant but also very challenging.

The writings of those two books of the Bible impacted me so much that I recall thinking, "If this is true, then this is the most dynamic, most exciting, most amazing thing in the whole wide world." But that's where I left it. It became a thought that was never really far away, but one that I wasn't sure I wanted. You see, I was so fed up with church on a Sunday that I was plotting and planning in my head how to get out of going any more. It was only the risk of hurting my family and friends that kept me attending. I can't even begin to imagine what my parents would have said if they had known. They were loving but strict and I know that I would have been forced to go until I was considered an adult or no longer living under their roof. Fortunately, it never came to that!

One Saturday afternoon we were visiting an uncle and his family. My older and very kind cousin, Ian, shared with my parents about some events that he had been going to. They were held in a barn, on a farm, on the Staffordshire/Derbyshire border and were led by two young brothers. There were weekly Saturday evening meetings and, on Bank Holiday weekends, there was the option of camping on the farm for the whole weekend.

That particular night, Ian offered to take me and ensure I got home safely, providing I could be excused from helping with the milking of our cows that night. It was with bated breath that I waited for my parents' response, not because I wanted to go to a Christian event but I didn't want to help milk the cows. When they said I could go I was overjoyed. What I didn't expect was to see hundreds of young people, teenagers, 20-somethings and a few slightly older getting out of their cars as we arrived.

There was such joy; I heard so much laughter and everyone seemed to be hugging one another. It appeared that they had all wanted to come by choice and not obligation. I loved it.

The worship was contemporary, with young people playing guitars. Someone spoke about Jesus and read a portion from the Bible. It was exciting and understandable. Families from our local town attended, so lifts were arranged and from that day Saturday became the highlight of my week. The 'Barn Rallies', as they were called, couldn't come around quickly enough for me. I was hearing everything against the background of my freshly learnt studies of the Gospel of Luke and the Acts of the Apostles and it all made sense. It was very early on in my attending these events that I received Jesus by faith into my life. It wasn't a public event but I know that at some point I prayed a prayer that went something like this: "Lord Jesus I am really sorry for the things I have done wrong in my life and I ask You to forgive me. I choose to turn away from everything I know is wrong and thank You that when You died on the cross You did it so that I could be forgiven. I accept that forgiveness and ask You to come into my life."

Although I can't remember the exact day, I know that the day I first went to the 'Barn Rally' I hadn't asked Jesus to be my Saviour. Within a year, I knew that if I had been the only person alive on the day of His crucifixion He would still have died...just for me! I would have been 16 years old at the time, and this event meant that I never had to tell my parents that I had wanted to leave church.

God's hand had been on me from before I was born, even in my mother's womb, and the effects of a praying family were now evident in my life.

My character is such that if a thing is worth doing then it's worth doing well, so I was out for 'the works.' I didn't just want to sing about what Jesus did two thousand years ago, I wanted it to be real in my life now. I didn't just want to read about the Acts of the Apostles, I wanted to live it now. This must have been annoying, and I expect I was a real pain to quite a number of people — so full of good ideas about what needed to change at church and in other situations. I was yet to learn about them needing to be 'God ideas' not good ideas. I was so open about my faith, and the hunger inside me to learn more, but wasn't expecting the response of some of the people who I loved dearly. It really knocked me back when I was told that I had gone 'all religious' when I used to be such fun. This caused me to withdraw.

Soon after this, some of the people from the 'Barn Rally' went away for a weekend to a Christian retreat centre in Shropshire. It was a new experience for me to be away without any family and I loved most of it. On the first evening, however, when we had all gathered in the lounge to worship, someone started to speak in a strange way. It really frightened me. What I didn't know then, was that this was one of the gifts of the Holy Spirit.

It was so alien to anything I had ever experienced and if I could have got out of that room I would have bolted all the way down the long drive - darkness or no darkness. Because I didn't know who to talk to about this, I said nothing and withdrew further.

One evening, when 17 or 18 years old, I was helping dad milk the cows. My brother Michael was sitting on something high off the ground so that he was safe from the moving animals when I stood in front of him and started to tell him about the decision I had made to give my life to Jesus. It is as clear in my mind as if it was yesterday. I can hear myself saying to him, "This is the biggest decision you can make with your life and it's the best decision you will ever make and because I love you so much, I want you to make that decision for yourself. Don't ever forget."

That was my first evangelistic talk and I can joyfully say that he did go on to make his own personal decision and he is a precious man of God, my brother and my friend.

Other than at the Saturday night events and at church, I chose to keep my faith from others. In private, though, I tried to seek God more. Try is the correct word: I would sit with an open Bible and just stare at the words that seemed so difficult to understand. I found it so hard to read the Bible or pray. There was a notion inside me that this was the right thing to do but only to gain what I thought would be God's approval. It was all out of duty and there was no desire in me for these practices.

I left school just before turning 16 and went straight to work in an office. The company arranged for me to attend college on day release to learn secretarial skills.

It was also around this time that I met Alan who had grown up nearby, although our paths had never crossed until then. My parents and Ruth all knew his father and uncle because Ruth worked alongside them. From the moment I saw him there was a lot I liked about Alan.

He arrived in a little sports car, parked in the manager's reserved parking place and jumped out. He was tall, dark and very handsome, wearing a brown suit and stripy cream and brown tie. I shouted to the girl in the next office, "You've just got to come and see this...but remember, I saw him first!" The manager asked me to type the letter to offer him a position of employment at the works and I was delighted.

Many things were happening quickly. I'd made the decision to follow Jesus but wasn't sure how to, so I was trying to be what I thought a Christian should be. At the same time, having been very immature and unworldly, I was exploring friendships in the new context of work and college.

I was quite mixed up really, trying to live up to the various standards I thought everyone expected of me. Everything I did was a performance, seeking approval from whoever I was with. One amazing thing I held on to was this: I was clear that I needed to marry someone who was also a Christian because somewhere deep in my being I knew that this was going to really matter. Alan was there in the background at work and we would occasionally speak but nothing more developed for quite a while.

It was during this time that I was asked to take part in a Young Farmers' event. It was to be a debate about something to do with farming and I was selected to speak. As I have already shared, I had never been one to be in the limelight. Somehow, though, I agreed to speak at this Young Farmers' event and at the end one of the judges approached me and said something to the effect that I had a very special gift of communication and should consider public speaking.

It seemed such a ridiculous idea and I remember it because I thought it funny. In my wildest dreams I could never have imagined anyone being interested in anything I had to say, nor having the confidence to speak in public.

A new minister was appointed to our church who was married with a young family and very approachable. It gave me pleasure to assist with some administration for him in his role within the district. The idea of me being able to use what I had learnt at college felt good. Although I felt I could talk to him a little, I don't recall ever sharing anything personal about my commitment to try to follow Jesus.

I soaked up the teaching I received at the 'Barn Rallies' every Saturday. The weekly times of worship and teaching provided an oasis in which I could grow, both in faith and understanding. As a result, I felt like one person in that environment and another everywhere else. Despite living a sort of dual life I felt assured of my salvation and, inside, I started to get an itch that I couldn't scratch. It didn't take me long to realise that God was prompting me to be baptised.

As soon as this dawned on me, I read all the references I could find in the Bible and I was on a mission to be baptised.

It was as though I suddenly became aware of the third person of the Trinity — the Holy Spirit — and although He was referred to within our services, I never heard anyone teach on Him. Any passages that I could find in my Bible that spoke of the Holy Spirit I would read over and over.

I have vivid memories of walking up and down the cowsheds following my dad as he milked the cows. I wanted to gain knowledge about the Holy Spirit so would ask him question after question. The desire to be baptised had stirred up such a deep thirst. Whilst not fully understanding, I felt sure that I needed to publicly demonstrate the decision I had made a couple of years earlier to follow Jesus by being baptised with total immersion in water. Naturally, having been christened as a baby, I was concerned about how my parents would react as our tradition didn't allow for doing it again. However, such was the sense inside me that this was something I needed to do; and on 27th August, 1973, during the Bank Holiday weekend at the 'Barn Rally' I was baptised in the River Dove. The only record I have is a little photo that someone gave to me some years later. It was a precious experience and I felt it sealed something inside me. I had a dynamic passion within me for life like the Acts of the Apostles, but outside of the 'Barn Rally' community I felt I had no one to share this with.

Around this time, Alan started to talk to me a little whenever he came across to the offices. He began doing some electrical work for my dad on the farm and so we would see something of one another there too.

He also did some electrical work at the church and was making himself very accessible including offering me lifts home after work. I knew that I was growing more and more fond of him. Many things attracted me in what I both saw and heard. The managers at the works spoke of his character and integrity and gave him a full set of security keys.

The only snag was this conviction that I should marry someone who would have the same desire to commit their life to following Jesus Christ, someone who would share my faith and that I could grow with.

There was a danger that if I spent more time with Alan, I would fall head over heels! I did speak with our minister about this and he suggested I ask Alan about whether he was open to the Christian faith. Sadly, I didn't follow this through because I didn't know how to. Instead, I invited him to church and at the same time he asked me to go on a date. We did both. Our first date was Easter Tuesday 1974 and the following Sunday Alan came to church. He started a journey of discovery about Jesus and was helped enormously by our minister, who visited Alan at his home a number of times to share the gospel and lead him through to salvation. By this time I was hopelessly in love and, with God's hand firmly on the two of us, we married on 4th October 1975.

It was the purity of God's love
that started the process of unlocking
and dealing with the hurt and pain.

Chapter Two
The Awakening

Alan and I were now married, happily living in our new home and adjusting to life together. Whilst we were attending what had become home church for both of us, we didn't grow in our faith. We attended services twice every Sunday but I was living no differently than before my commitment to Jesus and baptism. In fact, there was a lot of frustration inside me and I didn't know then that frustration is a form of buried anger.

There were things going on both in the workplace and extended family that were challenging. I felt very immature and ill-equipped to deal with these issues. Instead of talking things through I kept it all to myself. In addition, the full gospel weekly 'Barn Rallies' had ceased, leaving a deep void that wasn't being filled by church services. I was spiritually dry and struggling to read my Bible or pray.

On the surface, the majority of the time I was happy; however, deep inside was a different feeling. I experienced further inappropriate acts which resulted in me becoming one very mixed-up young woman holding on to stuff that, with hindsight, I should have brought into the open. I knew I was trying to perform to meet approval and acceptance wherever I was. Aware of my character flaws, my frustration was mainly taken out on Alan.

I was looking for him to be the perfect person who would either change or accommodate my imperfections and make me happy. I was looking to him to heal the buried pain, to set me free from the sense of shame that I was now carrying, that somehow these inappropriate acts were my fault. Alan, obviously, couldn't do that so felt he was failing me. God's hand was certainly on us and holding our marriage together — eventually we came through those days stronger.

Our precious son, Philip, was born in September 1977 and it was a time of great joy. The pregnancy and delivery had not been easy and my health was extremely delicate. To make matters worse, Philip had a knot in the umbilical cord which was wrapped around his neck. The delivery left me extremely scarred physically and mentally. Even so, those early days of our son's life are full of many happy memories with the making of new friends and both of us loving being parents. I was really unwell with all sorts of minor issues which affected our day-to-day lives. I suffered a degree of post-natal depression and I think the change of lifestyle from the freedom and activity of living on a farm to being in a small house, on a housing estate, didn't help.

Philip needed surgery when he was just two years old. Being only young myself, I didn't know how to handle the emotions that I was feeling over the operation. We had to admit him to the children's ward of the hospital where there were no facilities for parents. We were told to leave him and go home!

As you can imagine, to walk away from your child at such a time is now unthinkable, but we had no alternative.

When we visited for short periods, in the days following his surgery, he would turn his face away from us. We struggled with the pain and both felt very alone. We didn't have a network of support and God felt a million miles away.

I was still finding it hard to pray or read my Bible so I didn't. I really didn't want to attend any midweek activity at our church. Inside me, I felt that I had lost connection with God. Even though I had the assurance of Jesus being my Saviour, that dynamic passion of my teens had evaporated. On top of shame from my earlier years, I carried a further sense of guilt and shame about losing my passion for Jesus.

The years unfolded with Alan working extremely long hours and me working part-time with our parents providing childcare. I was struggling with all sorts of health problems: low blood pressure, bouts of low blood sugar levels, migraines and overwhelming weariness. There were times when I felt dizzy and faint often thinking I would pass out. Most of the time, I felt I was performing to please both God and people. No matter how hard I tried, I still could not connect with God, His Word (the Bible) or pray; it all became a sham simply adding to the guilt and shame.

When we discovered I was pregnant in 1981, we were overjoyed but extremely apprehensive, so decided that I should see a gynaecologist privately. This did give us some peace, but underneath I was still anxious about the pregnancy. Would it be like when Philip was born? Would I survive the birth? Would the baby survive? All valid questions based on the earlier pregnancy and delivery I had experienced.

Around this time, a new minister was appointed to our church. There was something different about Gilbert and his wife, Sylvia. When they preached they brought everything to life and when they prayed I felt their connection with God. They radiated joy and I would find myself looking at their faces and wanting that same thing for myself. I appeared happy but happiness depends on circumstances. They carried joy which I now understand is a gift from God. I loved their visits to our home. I felt they were people who listened but did not judge. This was significant to me as I was able to open up and share some of my fears and concerns about the pregnancy and delivery. I remember when he prayed with me for the pregnancy and safe delivery, I experienced a deep sense of peace. Both were fulfilled when our precious daughter, Charlotte, was born in April 1982, and there was a renewed stirring in me for the things of God.

A few months later, a change of minister was announced in our church and I thought the bottom had dropped out of my world.

The first Sunday I heard Derek, the new minister preach, he carried the same joy, peace and ability to bring the word of God through the Bible alive. I couldn't get enough exposure to his preaching, leading of worship and midweek group. The downside was that I felt he could read my thoughts — it was as if he had been listening in somehow! When he spoke, I felt like he was looking at me and I wanted to avert my gaze. It was a weird time of wanting to be where he was expounding the Word through the Bible, but hiding because I felt I was being exposed as a sham — one thing to the family and church family but another elsewhere.

Charlotte was taken seriously ill at ten months with a raging temperature and I couldn't get her to wake up. I recall getting into the back of an ambulance with her and all I could think was she's going to die. I cried out on the inside, "Please God don't let her die!" I don't know who rang who, or what was going on in the background, all I know is that when the ambulance arrived at the hospital Derek was already there waiting. I felt the security of his presence. After greeting me he asked could he anoint her with oil, which he did quickly, as we were being ushered into the hospital. Whatever anyone could do I would have agreed to in order to save our baby girl's life. I felt a deep sense of peace and calmness spread over me replacing the panic and helplessness. I remember sitting in the room holding her in my arms and saying in my inner thoughts, "God, I will give her to you if you let her live."

At that point I hadn't realised that God had given her to us!

Charlotte made a wonderful recovery and I never forgot the naïve but honest statement I made to God. Immediately after this, I found myself praying more often with mostly me-centred prayers. I started daily Bible reading notes and stuck to them some of the time. I made a priority of attending services and the midweek group and started to try and sort my attitudes out. I wasn't sure I liked myself at all. I was frustrated on the inside, lacking in patience and generally had a bad attitude. I could flare up in anger at the push of a button — usually with my gracious and loving husband or one of the children. I couldn't work out what was wrong with me. I had it all; a loving family, a wonderful husband, precious children, lovely home and a good career but inside I carried so much guilt, shame and anger. I felt I was living a 'performance to please' kind of life and was frustrated with Alan as he didn't seem to realise what I was feeling or how I was thinking. I now realise that he was very aware and that all I was doing was making him feel inadequate.

My health had stabilised somewhat, although I would get very bad migraines on a fairly regular basis. I was promoted at work and found great pleasure from the identity it gave me and I threw myself into my career.

I was loving the teaching that Derek was bringing. It was like the teaching from my teens, but now I was older I could enjoy the passages from the Bible and allow them to affect me.

I was challenged by one teaching he brought on forgiveness. I knew that there were a number of people that I wasn't in a good relationship with.

In particular, one lady sprang to mind and I knew I needed to ask her forgiveness before I could move on. Looking back, I can see how the Holy Spirit was at work convicting, not condemning, and causing me to act.

My temper was not good. I recall three episodes that are etched in my memory but want to point out that these episodes have all been wiped clean away through Jesus. On one occasion, my family and I were sitting at our pine kitchen table when something rose in me so powerfully that I tipped the table up. It frightened me as well as the children. Another occasion was when I was returning a plastic sealed container, which held sugar, back to the larder unit. I threw it with such strength through the open back door that it cleared the fence between us and our neighbours and hit their side wall. Alan took me calmly to sit down and, whilst I was sobbing, he walked round to next door and retrieved the container. Much later he joked that most people ask their neighbours for sugar, rather than throw sugar at them.

The third incident (these all fell in quick succession) was after having asked Philip to pick up a toy numerous times; I picked it up and broke it over my knee in rage. I have since asked forgiveness from him for that incident.

I share these not because I'm proud of them, quite the opposite, but it's important for you to understand the work that Jesus has done in my life.

Things were heating up! On the one hand, I was drinking in the Word of God like a thirsty child, while on the other my stinking attitudes seemed to be manifesting more.

At this point, Derek told us that he was organising teaching on the work and person of the Holy Spirit and it was going to be over a four-week period in March 1986 — I could not wait. Something was drawing me, and hovering at the back of my mind was my limited exposure to the third Person of the Trinity that I experienced in my teens.

Due to the hours Alan worked, I arranged for a babysitter to come for the four evenings. I was really looking forward to these sessions. The first three were so instructive and I learnt so much about the Holy Spirit. Then, on fourth evening, there was a guest speaker alongside Derek. It was a hectic day at work and I started to develop a migraine. By the time I had picked the children up, prepared and served them their evening meal, I felt so unwell that I was contemplating not going. The problem (or good thing) was I did not want to upset the babysitting arrangement or cancel travelling with my uncle and aunt. Reluctantly, and feeling quite unwell, I went. There were a good number of people present and the guest speaker began by saying, "I believe there is someone here tonight who has a migraine and is feeling quite unwell." He went on to say that God was present and wanted to heal that person from migraines.

It got my attention but I honestly thought that with so many people in the room it was very likely that there would be others beside me who had a migraine. I confess, I was very sceptical about what he had said.

He went on to explain about the gifts of the Holy Spirit and why believers should exercise these gifts.

Before long, I found myself caught up with the well-presented teaching.

As the evening drew to a close, Derek invited anyone who would like prayer to join him and the guest speaker in another room. Trays of refreshments were brought round; I happily took a cup of tea noting that my uncle and aunt were engaged chatting to others while I was hoping they would soon be ready to go as I just wanted to get back home. Suddenly, I realised that at some point during the teaching, my head had stopped hurting and my eyesight had improved. I felt better — and I have not had migraines since. Around the same time as grasping this, Derek's wife, Sue, came out of the kitchen, took my unfinished cup of tea from me, and merely said, "Anne you need to go through for prayer. She gently guided me towards the door of the smaller room and, obediently, I went because this was such an out of character thing for her to do. I felt I couldn't resist.

As soon as I stepped into the room, I encountered a tangible presence that I had not experienced before. I noticed that Derek and the guest speaker were standing praying with someone so I sat quietly and waited a few minutes. As this lady started to leave the room I stood up.

At that moment, I had an experience that I find difficult to explain: as I took a step forward to where the two men were standing, I gently fell to the ground, backwards and without pain. I was aware that I was lying on the ground and was conscious throughout the whole experience.

ANNE DONALDSON

Initially, I felt like I should be under the ground not lying on it as I was so aware of the rubbish inside me.

Then in a split second it felt like I had a washing machine working inside me cleansing away all the accumulated rubbish. I experienced waves of peace, joy and love flowing up and down my body. Wave upon wave. I felt that I could float above the ground because of the sense of freedom and lightness that surged through me. I just lay there on my back and relished every second of this experience. It was, and is, beyond description but it is as real to me today as it was that evening.

After what seemed like a long time, but apparently it was only a short time, the guest speaker knelt beside where I was lying and simply said, "God has called you to be His witness and preach His Word in Jerusalem, in Judea, in Samaria, and the nations of the world." Derek witnessed this and played a significant part in encouraging me to respond to this prophetic call.

Eventually, I got back on my feet and without any further prayer, I left the room. I found my uncle and aunt and we made our way home. I didn't know what had hit me. All I knew was that it was so good, so very good and the feelings inside were so different.

I can only liken it to when you have your hair done and you don't want to go to bed and lie down because you know that in the morning your hair won't look as good as when the hairdresser has done it! I was concerned that if I went to bed that night I would wake up the next morning with the same sense of oppression, bad attitudes and heaviness that I so often woke up with.

When I got home, Alan and the children were sound asleep in bed. Although it was late for me, I chose to sit for quite a long time and savour every moment.

I knew something big had happened; I knew it was something to do with the person of the Holy Spirit. I knew I wanted more so I simply wallowed in the sense of His love, His peace and His presence, lingering until the early hours of the morning.

I finally went to bed and slept but as soon as I woke up I knew something massive had changed. The lightness in my spirit had not gone away and it never has once since that day. I needed to get the children ready for school and the childminder and then get myself ready for work but I wanted to speak with Derek. I rang him and it was only when he responded sleepily that I realised I had rung very early. With grace, he said that he would come to see me that afternoon after I had finished work at 3pm, so I dashed home to meet with him.

He took me through what had happened and started to relate the teaching I had received over the past few weeks in a way that had a personal application.

He was very clear on what the guest speaker had spoken over me, explaining that it was a prophetic word that he believed was from God. He offered to meet me again in a few days and, in the meantime, encouraged me to pray about how I should respond to this message from God. I hadn't a clue where this would lead but I knew that I needed to be mentored and he was willing to do this which delighted me.

He gave me a booklet about the Holy Spirit and speaking in tongues, which I had first encountered on the Christian retreat weekend in my teens. I read the booklet from cover to cover, over and over again, during the following days.

There was an awakening inside of me, a stirring for the things of God, a desire to read my Bible and see what it had to say in the Acts of the Apostles. I found myself talking in my head to God about what had happened, and was happening, to me and found a real sense of awareness of Him.

I felt like a different person. I had encountered the love of God in a way I hadn't experienced before and I felt warm and satisfied on the inside. It was the purity of God's love that started the process of unlocking and dealing with the hurt and pain resulting from the negative experiences from my earlier years.

When we met a few days later, Derek advised that if I wanted to follow what God had said to me, I first needed to believe it and then take appropriate action. Up to this point, my nervousness would not allow me to stand up and speak or even read from the Bible in church, and here was my minister recommending training to preach. It was a suggestion which seemed daunting at the time but not as daunting as it would have prior to my recent spiritual experience. He explained how things were done in our tradition. I would be given a 'note' to preach, meaning my training would be done under the supervision of a more mature preacher, accountable to the local church, ministers and existing preachers.

I immediately said, "Yes!" One of the things I have noticed is when something needs to change I don't wait, I just go for it. If God shows me something, I don't hesitate, I just do it.

So, I embarked on training which I found most challenging. There were four parts to the training spread over two years, followed by an exam after each part. I studied the Scriptures in depth and then I wrote an essay based on what I had studied. It was a time when God highlighted some of the misconceptions I had regarding Him. After getting quite upset following one tutorial, my tutor used the analogy that what was happening to me was like a rope being unwound. He said the rope was good but a used rope gets matted with wear and tear, impurities and even rust. As the rope was being unfurled, rust and dust were being knocked off and the rope was being re-plaited in a way that would make it stronger. I clung on to that image believing that my re-plaiting would be centred around Jesus.

I remember being asked by our senior minister to share with other preachers and leaders what had happened to me and how I had received the call to preach. To me, being called in such a dramatic and transforming way was normal but over the years I have come to realise the uniqueness of the call God has placed on my life. I recognised that I needed to have my own "Road to Damascus" experience for a couple of reasons!

Firstly, because of the way God has wired me and how I express myself required a dramatic experience.

Secondly, the transformation that took place from that moment could only be due to the indwelling, empowering presence of God, so I couldn't boast because it was all about Him, all because of Him and all for Him.

I noticed that I was changing from the inside out. I was able to look back at incidents that had hurt me or caused me shame. I was able to forgive the perpetrators and eventually myself. My attitudes were changing. The anger had gone although some frustrations remained.

At that time in my life, I did not fully understand the transaction that had taken place at my salvation, that I had a new life and was a new creation. I understood the fullness of God in me but did not know how to apply it to my life. The Bible tells us how our sin is removed from us through the death of Jesus. A couple of meaningful passages from the Bible for me are:

> *"As far as the east is from the west, So far has He removed our transgressions [sins] from us."*

> **Psalm 103:12 (NKJV)**

> *and;*

> *"You [God] will cast all our sins into the depths of the sea."*

> **Micah 7:19 (NKJV).**

Once we accept that we have been forgiven through what Jesus has done for us, it is important that we forgive ourselves. Our sins have been cast into the depths of the sea — and we must not go fishing.

As far as the east is from the west they have been removed. They are gone forever!

I was given a mature supervisor, Tony, to help train, nurture, guide and encourage me in the way to prepare and deliver an act of worship. He was a friend before this time and remains so.

Looking back, I see how God surrounded me with the right people at this critical time and I thank Him for them being part of my walk of faith. Our lovely minister, Derek, who brought me through this period in the early 1980s, has since died but his legacy lives on for God's glory.

Our marriage was saved, I believe, when I came to the realisation that I needed wholeness through Jesus, and Alan could not make up what was lacking in me. I recognised that the expectations I put on Alan were wrong. I turned to Jesus to heal me, set me free and complete all that was missing inside. It was a dramatic transformation, however, it is an on-going process. At this point in my testimony I was still struggling with my identity.

I learnt many hard lessons during those early years of preaching, lessons that have equipped me for what God is doing now. I must have made so many mistakes and unwittingly caused hurt. I was so full of passion and zeal for Jesus and what He had done for me, a passion and zeal that has grown and matured.

I started to see depth of meaning in Bible passages that had previously been just words; good words and familiar words but it was as if these words became a personal message to me from God.

I received them as promises I needed to hold on to, encouragement on a day when I needed it or a loving correction. If God revealed something to me through His Word, that I needed to apply to my life, then I did it. I was not going to waste time or mess around. If God spoke to me, I trusted and responded.

I recall going to preach one Sunday morning: I arrived early and was greeted warmly by the church steward who took me to wait in a room at the rear of the church. After general conversation the elderly gentleman said, "So, what's God been saying to you this week?" He will never know how he was used that morning on this side of eternity. I spluttered something dismissive and changed the flow of conversation, but I tell you what, on the way home I metaphorically laid myself before God and asked Him to teach me how to listen, to hear and to receive what He wanted to communicate.

I have never heard the audible voice of God but I now definitely hear Him speak directly to me in my inner being. A friend calls them 'loud thoughts'. As I started to discern God was saying to me and applying it in my life, I noticed many good changes taking place in me — things that needed to change dramatically.

Even though God was working powerfully in my life, I was still living a different life in the workplace. I can assure you at this time no one who I worked with would have known that I was going through a spiritual transformation of learning to listen to God and applying to my life the truths I was discovering. I am saddened that I was not a witness in the workplace, merely giving them grounds to believe that Christians are hypocrites.

Our lives can be a dynamic testimony of the power of God at work in our hearts.

Chapter Three

Fruit and Gifts

I had accepted all my life that God existed. I knew that God so loved the world that He gave His only Son and now rather than being grouped as part of the world that He loves, I was feeling His love in a unique way and not just part of a collective. I sensed God's love for me in a personal way and recall reading Isaiah 43:1:

> *"I have redeemed you. I have called you by your name. You are Mine."*

> **Isaiah 43:1 (NKJV)**

God knows me. He calls me by name. I am a uniquely made person who God loves and knows. It was a revelation taking that knowledge from intellect to a deeper level.

One of the things I needed to explore at this time was exactly who the Holy Spirit is. I knew that He is a person of the Godhead, a term to describe the Trinity: Father, Son and Holy Spirit. But what I did not know then was that He is co-equal within the Godhead. I had this misguided idea that He is like some sort of 'tag-on' to God the Father and Jesus Christ the Son; thus completely missing the equality within the Trinity. I had a lot to relearn.

I grasped very quickly that He is holy and, if where He is becomes holy, then that means my body is holy and it should not be abused by myself or others. As I continued to understand and apply what I was learning, I recognised that He is life-giving and brings healing both in our relationship with God and in our minds and bodies. It is one of the works of the Holy Spirit to clean up our internal mess and that was something I had been trying to do by myself and failing.

In my late 30s, life was generally good: Alan and I had bought, and enjoyed renovating, our new home; family life was settled; we were fortunate to have incredible holiday times together; I had moved to a new workplace and I was enjoying my career. Most Sundays I was out preaching and God was able to use whatever I was able to offer, no matter how immature it was at that time.

Despite the significant changes that had taken place following my encounter with the Holy Spirit, there were still key areas of my life that needed sorting. My identity was not founded in God. I was still seeking significance and approval through what the world had to offer but God hadn't done with me yet!

The ongoing work of God in my life was causing me to examine my attitudes and relationships further. In a situation where previously I would have reacted badly, I noticed myself choosing to react differently.

Over an extensive period of months, I found myself writing letters, making phone calls, seeking individuals to ask for their forgiveness and to explain changes in decisions and choices that I had made previously.

There was quite a clean-up operation taking place at pace and there seemed to be a lot to do.

I love cooking and baking and one of my specialities is a hazelnut meringue gateau. One of the secrets of making a good meringue is to eliminate all impurities and even though you have washed, dried and put away clean utensils after previous use, it is important to start making a meringue in a freshly washed bowl with freshly washed utensils. In this simple act, God showed me how I needed to constantly turn to Him for cleansing. Yes, at the point of my salvation, I was washed clean through the death of Jesus on the cross and by His blood spilt for me but then there is the ongoing cleansing known as sanctification. To use a metaphor, it's keeping the utensils clean so that the air being incorporated into the meringue can do its job. I quickly understood that this ongoing cleansing was making a big difference in the way I thought and acted.

People close to me began to see the changes and were asking what had happened. I was unsure how to share what had occurred because it required terminology that I didn't understand. Had I been filled with the Holy Spirit or baptised in the Holy Spirit? I had received Jesus into my life at the point of salvation, so was a little confused as to what this latest experience had been.

It had been a dramatic event that brought in some remarkable changes in me.

I learnt that what had happened was not for thrills but to empower me to serve God's purposes, helping me work alongside Him within the life and ministry of the church.

Firstly, I recognised that before He could empower me, any known sin was to be repented (cleaning the bowl before making the meringue). Secondly, I needed to have faith in Jesus Christ with the desire that my life should be evidence of His resurrection.

For me, this revelation and encounter of the Holy Spirit happened 14 years after becoming a believer. Within my memory, I had never had this explained to me or been taught about the person of the Holy Spirit in a clear and concise way. Nowadays, I love to share what I have learnt with others so that they don't have to struggle in the way I did.

Having studied Luke's Gospel for my O Levels, and from further reading of Luke 3, I knew that Jesus was a man completely filled with the Spirit of God and how the Spirit of God descended on Him in bodily form at His baptism. He returned from the River Jordan full of the Holy Spirit and was then led by the Spirit into the desert, returning to Galilee in the power of the Holy Spirit. What I read was that Jesus Himself was filled, baptised, absorbed, overwhelmed, immersed, plunged and totally soaked in the Spirit of God.

Jesus also taught how the Holy Spirit would come for us.

In John 7:37-38, it explains how, on the last day of a feast, Jesus stood up and proclaimed to the people:

"If anyone is thirsty let him come to Me and drink. Whoever believes in Me, as the scripture has said, streams of living water will flow from within him."

John 7:37-38 (NIV)

I was beginning to see that because I live in Him and He in me, this river would flow out of me. In addition, Jesus is saying that the river will flow, bringing life, fruitfulness and healing to ourselves and others. I knew that what I had experienced and continued to need was healing from the inside out.

I kept reading the opening passage of the Acts of the Apostles and seeing things with fresh insight. Just before He ascended into Heaven, Jesus promised His disciples that they would receive power when the Holy Spirit came on them and they had to wait another ten days. On the day of Pentecost (Acts 2), the disciples were filled with the Holy Spirit and began to speak in other tongues as the Spirit enabled them. Following my experience of being baptised in the Holy Spirit, I had the ability to speak in tongues but I didn't straight away. Soon after, this became clear to me when I heard some people talking in Russian on a television programme.

It occurred to me that although the words made no sense to me this did not mean it wasn't communication! I needed to exercise faith by starting to make sounds that didn't make sense. Nevertheless, this was my gift from the Holy Spirit and it started with just one syllable repeating the same sound over and over until I gradually found more sounds and so the gift developed.

I began using the gift of tongues more and more but it was usually on my own whilst driving to and from work each day.

However, I found that spending approximately fifteen minutes each journey was releasing something inside me and I firmly believe that exercising the gift in this way brought some of those healing changes into my life.

I wanted to explore hearing God for myself more and more. I recall reading a book that helped me enormously. It was written by someone who had been brought up as a Christian but had an encounter that transformed his understanding of the work and person of the Holy Spirit highlighting how God speaks to us today. I used notes from my reading, from the journaling I was doing, from things I had learnt from our minister's teaching and truths understood as I read the Bible for myself. I learnt very early on the difference between the fruit of the Spirit and the gifts of the Spirit. It was as if what had happened to me was a practical demonstration of this difference.

The fruit of the Spirit is detailed in Galatians 5:22-23:

> *"The fruit of the Spirit is love, joy, peace, patience, kindness, goodness, faithfulness, gentleness and self-control."*

Galatians 5:22-23 (NIV)

Fruit develops over time and gifts need to be exercised by faith.

Our son, Philip, had a holiday job working at a soft fruit farm where he would prune the canes and prepare the plants for fruiting.

It was one day when taking him to work that I sensed God say to me that only strawberries could grow on strawberry plants and only raspberries could grow on raspberry canes. It was an obvious thing but He continued to direct my thoughts.

I realised that what causes the fruit to form and then develop is the need for an insect to cause fertilisation. The coming together of the pollen on the insect with the stigma of the plant results in fruit. In the same way as I was opening my inner self, increasingly to the presence of God, so the very DNA of who Jesus is was causing my spirit to reproduce His nature within me: the fruit of the Spirit. For years, whilst I had been trying to be loving, joyful and peaceful I couldn't achieve this alone. It had to be a work from within, through the Holy Spirit, and the changes within me were the result of that powerful encounter with God. His love, His joy and His peace were now becoming more evident in and through my life.

The fruit of the Spirit is the very nature of God and is the result of encounters with Him that lead us into an ongoing experience. The fruit, being displayed in our lives, becomes the lifestyle that delights God which brings consistency to our attitudes and behaviour because God is unchanging. What God was doing in me was offering me His unchanging nature so that His nature displayed through me was starting to be more constant. I noticed that the fruit of the Spirit was starting to show up in situations and in my dealings with other people, whilst at the same time I was asking God to develop wisdom in me.

From the late 1980s and throughout the 90s I was receiving invitations to preach further afield and in various denominational churches. One day, I was reading Exodus 33 and reached verses 12–23 when I had another of those lightbulb moments. I was reading where Moses said to God something along the lines of, "If Your presence doesn't go with us, then what is there to distinguish us from all the other people?" It changed me in a flash. This statement has become one of the straplines for my life: If God's presence isn't with me then should I be doing it? The presence of God is the place from which we should conduct everything we do.

I started to hear comments like 'You are a breath of fresh air,' and understood that what they were perceiving was the very breath of God's presence flowing through what I was sharing as I preached. Our lives can be a dynamic testimony of the power of God at work in our hearts. I was so aware of being transformed from the inside and this became my ongoing prayer. As I've already stated, there was a tremendous refining going on and it was as if I was being sifted like flour — another baking analogy. I felt that not only my thoughts, actions and attitudes were being sifted but that the gauge in the sieve was getting increasingly smaller.

Another comment I would hear was, "You are always smiling and happy!" This was a lovely reflection of what people saw and perceived. It was joy that I was carrying and spilled out most of the time through smiles and happiness. Joy, however, is so very different to happiness.

I have a permanent joy bubbling inside even when things are tough and I'm not feeling happy. Joy is a natural overflow of the presence of Jesus in our lives.

In Isaiah 61:3 (NKJV) it tells how God exchanges discouragement and oppression with joy so we can rejoice and praise. In the same chapter, verse ten, the writer says that:

"I will greatly rejoice in the Lord, my soul shall be joyful in my God". Why? "For He has clothed me with the garments of salvation, He has covered me with the robe of righteousness."

Isaiah 61:10 (NKJV)

How can I not be joyful? Jesus has taken the dirty old rags of my old life and exchanged them for the beautiful clothes of salvation and covered me with the robe of righteousness. What God sees when He looks at me is the beauty of His Son and His righteousness. What an exchange! I began to see myself differently because of this understanding, seeing myself dressed in a beauty that Jesus clothed me with. I started to understand how, when God looks at me, He sees that beauty. As a result of this, my joy became full through experiencing the joy of Jesus within me.

I love John's Gospel and the things that John writes are amazing. In John 15:11 he writes:

"These things I have spoken to you, that My joy may remain in you, and that your joy may be full."

John 15:11 (NKJV)

ANNE DONALDSON

What things has Jesus spoken to me? He has spoken about abiding, remaining and living in His love. Living day by day, moment by moment in His presence and love brings fullness of joy!

Joy is a quality of character that is possessed and given only by God. It is rooted in my relationship with the Holy Spirit and is part of the fruit of the Holy Spirit. It was years before I was taught and understood that it is a powerful tool for life: a tool that can disarm spiritual attack. Let me explain...

When Alan is working manually, doing a project, he sometimes wears a tool belt around his waist. The belt has a number of pockets within its construction for different tools that he might need whilst in that situation. For example, different sized screwdrivers, pliers and other items. In a spiritual way, we have been given spiritual tools that we carry as part of who we are because of God's presence being in and with us. The fruit of the Spirit is a powerful tool that we have instant access to in any situation. Joy, along with the other eight qualities that make up the fruit of the Spirit (Galatians 5:22-23), is one of those tools that can disarm things like hopelessness, negative statements made against us, oppression and other circumstances we can find ourselves in where we feel under attack either emotionally or spiritually. If you have placed your trust in Jesus Christ, I can assure you that you are equipped with every tool you need for living as God intends you to have.

Another phrase often used about me was, "You are very confident." Whilst I knew that my confidence was in Him and because of Him, not in myself, others did not.

Those who had known me from childhood knew something big was taking place as I was no longer the crying child that would have given anything to get off the Sunday School Anniversary stage.

A statement I heard frequently was, "You must be a teacher in your profession." I was anything but! My O Level results had been passes in three subjects, which I still love today: religious studies, cookery and general science, and I only scraped through because of my enjoyment of them. I heard the comment about my being a teacher so often I dismissed it until God confirmed to me my calling to teach about Him and the Bible within the worldwide church.

During this period of finding truths, about discerning the voice of God, I kept simple notes and journals. I can't attribute what I learnt to any specific individual, writing or situation; I just recorded what I was receiving from God. I realised that God wants to communicate with us because He loves us and wants to reveal Himself to us. He desires intimacy with us, drawing us to Himself. He wants to share with us what is 'to be'. I discovered that He created us to hear His voice, rarely an audible voice, but generally an inner voice which speaks differently to each person. I know the way God speaks to me and know that it may be different from the way He speaks to you but what is important is that we each learn to recognise the voice of God. I realised that to recognise God speaking to me I needed to engage in personal times of worship and adoration, to develop an intimate relationship with Him.

As you may remember, in our early years of marriage, Alan and I worked for the same company.

Sometimes people would carry so-called messages from Alan to me as a joke. As they shared with me what Alan was supposed to be saying I would just laugh and dismiss the message because I knew it didn't carry the essence of who Alan is to me. Alternatively, I would accept the message because it carried the essence of our intimate relationship. In the same way, I know when a thought, a sensing or a statement carries the very essence of who God is to me. Learning to discern His voice is a process of growth that only comes through intimacy. I know that what He wants to speak to us about personally must line up and be consistent with His inspired Word in the Bible.

God wants to communicate with us because it is an integral part of who He is. He desires intimacy and relationship with us. He is a relational being and He created us to hear His voice. God wants to communicate with us because He wants to protect and provide for us. He wants us to benefit by receiving direction from Him because He knows what is best for each one of us. He has made us all unique and so He has a personal plan for each life that would bring us the most joy, fulfilment and purpose according to the nature He has given to each one of us. By now, I was experiencing such joy from the confidence that I was growing in that I came to an understanding that changing my agenda from my life to His would result in life in all its fullness.

God does speak to us through our thoughts but only through the renewed mind. It is because of Jesus, and the work of the Holy Spirit, that everyone who puts their trust in Jesus can have a renewed mind where the thoughts originate from Jesus Himself and line up with the written word of God as found in the Bible.

These thoughts and impressions are inspired by the Holy Spirit and are not based on background, attitudes or personal theology. They are based on Kingdom of God principles where the gifts of the Holy Spirit operate through love and the fruit of the Spirit is clearly evidenced.

Paul writing to the church in Corinth says:

> *"For who has known the mind of the Lord that he may instruct him? But we have the mind of Christ."*

> **1 Corinthians 2:16. (NKJV)**

So how does God speak to us today? This is an important part of my healing story. There are many and various methods of communication that God has used throughout history. We only have to read the Bible to see how He has spoken through the ancient biblical prophets, through Jesus, through the Holy Spirit, angels, dreams, visions and so on. I needed to be familiar with the ways God communicates because hearing God would affect my life so dramatically.

In Acts 9:4 we read how God spoke to Saul on the road to Damascus. On this occasion it was an audible voice because it says that the men who were with Saul heard the voice too but saw no one. In the Old Testament, Samuel heard the audible voice of God. In Acts 10 we read how Peter had a vision which communicated God's plan and direction to him. There are many examples in both the Old and New Testament of how God speaks through dreams.

For example, to Joseph, Jacob's son (Genesis 37) and to Joseph, who was married to Mary, the mother of Jesus (Matthew 2).

In John 1:48, we read how Jesus 'saw' Nathanael as a mental image. This is one of the ways God speaks to me: through mental images and also through sensing or receiving a strong impression. You can read in Acts 15:28 (NKJV) when the apostles needed to act on something they had sensed:

"For it seemed good to the Holy Spirit, and to us."

Acts 15:28 (NKJV)

Today, He speaks to us through the Bible, as well as all the above, through modern day prophets, through mental images, sensings or impressions. All these ways are biblically grounded and became part of my growth in both faith and identity.

As the 1990s progressed, wonderful things were happening. I was accepting God's love for me and this was changing me. As I gave Him my whole being — an ongoing process — He was making me complete. As a family, we celebrated with both Philip and Charlotte as they made, and shared publicly, their own commitment to Jesus and their being filled and empowered by the Holy Spirit.

I was so touched when Charlotte made her public commitment at the age of 12. She said, "Now I understand why you get so excited about God!"

I didn't realise that in our home my excitement about the things of God had become so evident.

Philip is much more like his dad and has a strong, unwavering sense of God in his life, but no bells and whistles.

Alan had his own experience of the Holy Spirit soon after me but in a totally different way. As Alan explained, God revealed Himself in a much gentler and longer way than my experience had been. That's another thing I love about God: He deals with each one of us in a unique way. The way He deals with me will probably be different from the way He deals with you. I express myself with 'flashing lights' passionately, and that's how He deals with me.

Yes, God was doing a great thing in me, in Alan and the children; however, I started to want more than what I was getting through church life: my own studies and prayer life, but didn't know where to find it.

We went as a family to Cliff College, a nearby Bible college, on one of their special weekends, which brought out yet more angry stuff that was buried inside me (not a nice journey for any of us as I remember). I can't recall what it was that caused an angry outburst but I do recollect the shame I felt as we arrived for this Christian event. Whilst there, I recall us singing the chorus: "Here I am, wholly available — as for me, I will serve the Lord"

Somehow, despite my angry outburst during the journey, I really meant every word I was singing. As I sang the words, it felt like I was sharing my heart with Jesus.

It had become a tradition to meet up with my father's brothers, their children and grandchildren on the first Saturday in May each year. This particular year, I think 1994, we met up at one of my cousin's homes just outside of Cambridge. After sharing lunch, we set off on a walk. I fell into step with two of my cousins, both of whom had come to faith in God through Jesus Christ. It was an absolute joy to walk and talk with them. They started to share about Christian events they had attended where they had received prayer ministry, a prophetic word, or heard great teaching. What they were describing was what was in my heart. This sounded exactly what I felt I needed.

All the way home, in the car that night, I was quiet but inside I was anything but quiet. I cried out to God to show me where I could go to link with others who desired God like I did, who wanted to grow spiritually and in their understanding of God. I wanted to be taught by Spirit-filled teachers, to move freely in and exercise the gifts of the Spirit, to both give and receive in ministry. I wanted the seed that had been planted in me whilst studying for my O Levels to burst and grow. I wanted to experience an Acts of the Apostles type of faith.

Be obedient even when you do not know where obedience may lead you.

Chapter Four
Learning Obedience

I was learning so much through the 1990s, discovering ever more of God's plan and purpose for living. I was growing more and gradually being transformed. Spiritual principles were being learnt and I was seeing changes in my life, my marriage, my family life on an ongoing basis.

I liken my growing relationship with the Lord to that of doing a jigsaw. If you don't do jigsaw puzzles forgive me, but if you do you will understand this.

Firstly, I sort the pieces. I separate the edge pieces from the rest and turn all the pieces upwards for the colours to show. Then I start by completing the edges to establish the boundaries which enables me to familiarise myself with the layout and colours. Initially, the jumbled pieces look predominately blue, yellow, green, red and brown, but when I start to assemble the pieces, I see there are many shades of each colour.

As I progress, I begin to recognise the exact shade needed for a particular part of the puzzle. The more time I spend familiarising myself with the picture, the more detail I see and the more intentional my selection of pieces to fit the place where I need to go next. This is like my relationship with God; the more time I spend looking at the various aspects of who He is, the more I familiarise myself with His divine attributes.

The deeper I grow in knowing Him, the deeper I know Him, the more I trust Him, the more I know His ways, the quicker I recognise His voice and the easier I can respond to His guidance.

I was learning that we can give mental assent to the gospel and yet not embrace or nurture it. What I mean by this is that we can agree with something in principle but not apply that principle to our personal situation. To apply what we believe is something that needs nurturing. It is this nurturing process that allows it to grow and develop so that we become more like Jesus.

It was reading the Bible that brought expansion into my life, enlarged my potential under God and was bringing me to a place where I was fulfilling the unique purpose of God for me.

Fruitfulness is a guaranteed by-product from studying and responding to God's Word in the Bible. His Word cannot be fruitless because His own life power is in it. I have read somewhere that seeds can lie dormant for centuries until the right conditions occur. Whilst dormant, they are not fruitful but inside there is the potential for fruitfulness. The day I received Jesus into my life, by faith, it was like a seed that had been planted needing the right conditions to grow, bloom and be fruitful. God was allowing situations to arise in my life that would lead me to seek the right conditions for the seed to grow.

It is a wonderful truth that one of the names of our God is the All Sufficient One, in Hebrew this is El Shaddai, as used in Genesis 17:1 (NKJV). He lacks nothing...but He does desire relationship.

I was really discovering that He Himself is a relational being. I could see one being within the Godhead (Father, Son and Holy Spirit), yet three persons in relationship.

God wants to be in relationship with us so much. He desires intimacy with us. Relationships are His masterplan. His idea is for man and woman to love one another, enjoy intimate relationship and develop this into family life. When family life works it is one of the most amazing things but when it doesn't it is one of the most painful. It is His idea for us to be part of the family of God, to relate to Him as a parent, with us showing that childlike trust enjoying spending time in His presence. Our problem is that we often carry the scars and wounds of earthly life due to broken relationships; and can include being abused emotionally or physically by those who should love us the most.

People can end up feeling unable to relate with God as a loving Father. Our identity gets distorted and we struggle with earthly relationships through this inaccurate perspective. This was never God's intention.

His intention is that we all are restored back into a wholesome loving relationship with Him and through the work of Jesus Christ on the cross we receive forgiveness and a new start. A new life of intimacy and trust with Him spills over into our earthly relationships. It's a relationship that is based on unconditional love, trust, understanding, honour and respect. Knowing this unconditional love of God, and growing in my identity as His child, affected the way I conducted myself more and more. What I didn't know then was that there was much more to be done!

There was a lot of joy throughout this time as the four of us grew and developed as a family in our faith. We were learning daily new truths and experiencing God's provision, protection, faithfulness, goodness and so much more. Throughout their teenage years, both our children were such a blessing, which they continue to be. Their faith, their subsequent choice of life partners, and now seeing their children grow in their own personal faith, is a rich gift in our lives.

I can remember one particular day as if it were only yesterday. I had been feeling under the weather and over-tired. When I woke up, I knew I could not go into work, which was unusual in itself. I stayed in bed and simply rested. As the morning wore on, I picked up a little book from our bookcase that had been a gift given to me for my 21st birthday by a family from our church. Until that day, I had never read it.

It was a collection of statements and I opened and read the following:

> *"And in this he showed me a little thing, the quantity of a hazelnut, lying in the palm of my hand, as it seemed. And it was as round as any ball. I looked upon it with the eye of my understanding, and thought, 'What may this be?' And it was answered generally thus, 'It is all that is made.' I marvelled how it might last, for I thought it might suddenly have fallen to nothing for littleness. And I was answered in my understanding: It lasts and ever shall, for God loves it. And so have all things their beginning by the love of God. In this little thing I saw three properties.*

The first is that God made it. The second that God loves it. And the third, that God keeps it."

– Julian of Norwich, Revelations of Divine Love

This statement touched me deeply. I just lay in bed and allowed this truth to penetrate beyond my mental capacity into my spirit. It was so simple: God made me, God loves me, God will keep and sustain me.

Let me repeat these statements praying that they will penetrate deep inside you as they did in me: God made you, God loves you and God will keep and sustain you. God chose me, He made me and He loves me greatly.

His love for me is not founded on my behaviour. His love for me, and you, is founded on who He is and that is why Jesus could die for us while we were still unaware of the sin in our lives. His love is not about your or my behaviour; our behaviour is not the criterion for receiving His love.

I knew that God was wanting to impart something deep into my understanding so, eventually, I turned to read my Bible notes for that day. It was the passage from Matthew 6:25-34 which in my Bible – the New King James Version – is headed 'Do not worry'.

I read this scripture as if for the first time. As I lay quietly in bed, I surrendered all worry and anxiety to God and received a peace and restoration. It was another of those milestone moments.

Reading through my prayer journal as I write this book has been so encouraging.

Because it is a journal that covers many decades, I can see how much I have grown spiritually over the years. Going back and reading about some of the issues I was struggling with at that time, and then reading on and seeing how God was guiding me, setting me free, healing, restoring, directing and revealing truths to me has been a joy. I needed to surrender worry and anxiety to God at that time. Reading on in the journal confirms the transaction that took place that day: I gave God my anxiety, He gave me His peace.

Soon after that Alan, myself and the children went to York for a holiday. While we were in York two very significant things happened: the first while we were visiting the Minster.

As tourists wandering around the building, I came to a display representing the events of Good Friday through to Easter Sunday and I experienced something where everything around me faded away and it was as if I entered into the display. It was strange but it had a profound spiritual impact on me.

The other thing was that I realised we were near to a well-known ministry centre and, having read about how this came into being, I wanted to visit and see for myself. I asked Alan if we could drive there and stay for the Friday night ministry event. We did, and having met the leader of this ministry he invited me to share from the front.

I recall many years ago, whilst on a course at our church, the illustration given was that at one time the person didn't want anything to do with leadership within the church — that was until they sensed and received a clear directional call from God.

Then, suddenly, it became the thing they most wanted to do with their life. I have experienced this so many times and it is so liberating! When the call, the directive, comes from God, by denying our own agenda and life plans, He (in the way only God can) causes us to have a passion, zeal and desire for the very thing that we previously couldn't imagine doing. It is so affirming and empowering, too.

Looking back to when I was 18 and asked to speak on behalf of the Young Farmers' Group, the transformation was 180 degrees. I had moved from a place of hating being in the spotlight, not wanting to say anything, to having the desire and God-given boldness to share the Good News about Jesus with everyone.

I quickly got a sense that God was calling me to ministry, so I spoke with our minister at that time, sharing as best I could, what I was sensing.

We met one evening later that week and it was an excellent time. I left knowing that something that had all the hallmarks of God was on the brink of happening. I believed I was being prepared and, at the same time, I was ready for this 'something'. Alan, my minister and I were the only ones who knew at that point and we took time to pray about whatever 'this' was.

A few weeks later, I met our minister again, and this time he said that he felt that I might be being asked by God to go into full-time ordained ministry. He shared that he was so happy to put me forward for consideration if Alan and I would pray about it and then get back to him. His parting words were strange and sounded like a warning.

He said that if I was agreeable to being put forward for ordination, he believed that nothing would stop the wheel turning. He was so positive that I would be recommended, and approved, that he told me to be certain before saying 'yes'.

I wasn't certain but I didn't know why. In the natural it seemed right. But I just knew that in the depth of my being that this wasn't what God was calling me to do. By listening to the inner voice, and the sense of the Holy Spirit, that I was able to be obedient to God. I went back to my minister and said, "No!"

I was grateful to both God and our minister for that experience because it taught me so much about obedience and listening for God's lead.

Deep within us all is a desire to know that your life can have impact, that there is a reason why we are here and that we are part of something bigger than ourselves. I was looking for something that gave me a sense of purpose and spiritual value. What I still had to grasp was that only God, as my Creator, could give me that. He was showing me that He alone is the only source of true significance. He is the one who knows the plans and purposes He has for us and these are good.

My career had developed and I was now working as an office manager at a public relations and advertising agency. A couple of weeks later, whilst I was at work, Philip, who was at home on exam revision, took a phone call from a lady inviting me to a meeting to pray about establishing a local group of a large international interdenominational ministry in our town.

I went along to that first prayer meeting and that evening, as the vision of the ministry was shared, I remember thinking that it sounded exactly what I had cried out to God for months earlier. We had a time of beautiful worship and then prayed. It is difficult to describe what happened during that short period of time but I knew that God was clearly calling me to be part of this ministry.

It was either just before or just after this prayer meeting that we, as a family, were on holiday in Ibiza. On the last morning of our holiday I got up early and went out on the balcony to read my Bible and daily study notes. After reading the passage allocated for that day, and because I was going to be celebrating my 40th birthday the weekend after our return, I looked ahead to the passage for the 15th August. I nearly jumped in the air with what I saw and read. Sandwiched between the pages for the 14th and 15th August was a picture of camels crossing a desert and a sentence from Deuteronomy 2:7:

"The Lord your God has blessed you in all the work of your hands. He has watched over your journey through this vast desert. These forty years the Lord your God has been with you, and you have not lacked anything."

Deuteronomy 2:7 (NIV)

I could hardly believe what I was seeing and reading. I felt I was receiving a 40th birthday card from the Lord Himself and the scars from my youth, regarding my birthday, were removed in an instant. God was healing me from inside.

There was a further sentence from Jeremiah 29:11:

"For I know the plans I have for you, declares the Lord, plans to prosper you and not to harm you, plans to give you hope and a future."

Jeremiah 29:11 (NIV)

Then a statement, written by the Scottish Theologian Sinclair Ferguson which read, "Be obedient even when you do not know where obedience may lead you."

That morning I received all of those sentences as a personal word. The first from Deuteronomy 2:7 felt like God was saying, "You have been wandering in the desert but it's okay because I've been watching over you and right there with you in all the 'stuff' but now it is time to move into the promises. Move out of the desert and into the oasis of my presence."

Through the Jeremiah word I felt He was saying, "It's time to let go of your plan for your life and yes, things might seem tough, but 'my plan' for you is to prosper and with 'my plan' you won't come to any harm."

The statement by Sinclair Ferguson was God saying to me, "You are going to have to really trust Me and simply follow in obedience." How true these words were to become. This was another milestone moment. I knew I was to get intentional and focused on what God was doing and saying to me.

I committed to being part of the new work of this ministry in my town.

I loved the new relationships with the ladies there and devoured every morsel of God's Word, presence and deeper revelation. He heard my cry and answered me.

I never looked back. I was like a sponge soaking up everything, learning to discern, how to exercise the gifts and entering into life-long friendships that are so precious I can't begin to describe. Our monthly prayer meetings were so exciting and never before had I been able to use those words together: prayer meeting and exciting! As we gathered to pray there was such an expectation of an encounter with God. We had the opportunity to pour out our worship in words using the gift of tongues and songs. All the while, we were privileged to hear Him speak through passages from the Bible, in pictures and through our sensing. These prayer meetings were a monthly highlight for me.

It was at my first Midlands' Conference of the ministry that all the delegates were given a card, which was beautifully crafted, and had the following written on it: "Blessed is she who believed, for there will be a fulfilment of those things told her from the Lord." The card, approaching 30 years old, stands proudly on my dressing table today.

I was learning to not only hear God's Word but how to live in it, and from it, as well as learning to hear God's voice and trust in it. My faith was increasing constantly and because I wanted to be more available for ministry I chose to lay down secular work in 1995. In fact, it wasn't a choice as such but a responding to God's lead. There was more learning during this process.

At that time, I was working in a very responsible management role, earning a good salary and enjoying the satisfaction of the work. I really believed that God had opened the way for me to work there.

One day I was in the kitchen area at work when I accidentally scalded myself with water from the newly-installed instant boiling water machine. The boiling water ran over the back of my hand, between thumb and forefinger, really hurting me. I ran the cold water tap over my hand but you could already see a large area of skin affected. I covered my scalded hand with my good hand and prayed healing in the name of Jesus. Asking for the skin to be healed and pain to go, I was truly believing that God would answer. After a few seconds, I removed the 'good' hand from the scalded hand and stood looking. There was no mark, burn, damaged skin, nothing — it was as new. This was the first time I experienced a physical healing, instant restoration of something that was damaged. I was in total awe at this event. From that time onwards, anything that happened within the family, I would pray in the name of Jesus, exercising faith.

One of my tasks at work was to interview potential administration staff and to organise temporary staff to cover staff holidays, sickness etc. One lady interviewed extremely well and she was appointed. We had an instant rapport and I enjoying working within the same team. One day, when I was making myself a hot drink in the kitchen area, she came up behind me and asked me if I was a Christian. I was so taken aback because I knew that to ask such a question she must herself be one.

This was the start of a lovely friendship, but sadly this beautiful woman had been hurt, damaged and betrayed so badly whilst still a young Christian that she turned her back on the church. We are still friends today; I still love her and pray for her. I shared with her that I was struggling with the compromise that I knew I would be expected to make if I was to continue to work in this environment. I was seriously thinking that after three years of working in this fulfilling role I needed to look for another job.

I was busy with responsibilities in my home with two children, preaching many Sundays, speaking at some mid-week church events and the growing commitment to the ministry I had volunteered with. Alan recognised, before I did, that I needed to be free from paid employment. He suggested it one day, but I did not really want to hear it, although inside I knew that this was how God was directing me. He wanted me to be fully available for ministry.

I kept wondering as to how would we afford to live on one salary especially with the children the ages they were? We were planning for Philip to go to university and knew that Charlotte, too, would benefit from university. It was a crazy idea to lay down my salary just as we were about to embark on one of the most expensive times of family life.

My thoughts would keep going back to that day I had rested and God had spoken to me about the passage from Matthew 6 and had exchanged my anxiety for His peace. Also, there was the 40th birthday card from God, as I came to call it.

I knew that His plans were good, so much better than mine, and so I started to consider leaving my role at a time that would cause the least disturbance to the company. As time passed, I felt more challenged to apply the truth from Matthew 6, to trust God and not my salary for provision for our family.

Being responsible for staff starting and leaving, I found myself musing about what would be the perfect day to hand my notice in. From an administrative point of view the perfect day would be when the 1st of the month was a Monday.

One day, when working in my office, I noticed that within a few weeks the 1st May was going to fall on a Monday. It was like a firework going off inside me. I was in no doubt that I was to lay down secular work completely and hand in my notice on that day in 1995. Just two days later, I was approached by a more senior leader in the international ministry to see if I would pray about going with her on a two-and-a-half week pioneering trip into the Ukraine, which was to be sometime in the autumn. Seeing God's perfect timing, Alan and I were affirmed by the way this all unfolded.

During the early 90s, I had been given a number of prophetic words by people who sensed that God was calling me to minister in Eastern Europe. I was unsure about this. There were a few fears in me: I had a fear of flying, fear of being away from home and a fear of dangers whilst in a different country. It was going to really take me out of my comfort zone.

The ministry in Great Britain had the oversight of the Ukraine with a view to pioneering and planting new groups there. We were to develop relationships with the bishops and pastors whilst appointing leaders over the new groups. I really felt that it would be an amazing privilege to be involved in this but I had a number of concerns about going and being away from the home and family. But even the small details were smoothed out and, in obedience, I went to the Ukraine on 13th October 1995...my first international trip!

I love the way God shows me things that need dealing with just through the day-to-day situations. During the period of time between June, when I finished work, and October I had an identity crisis. I had enjoyed my career but never stopped and realised how much of my identity was wrapped up in my role and presentation. I had always worn a suit and high heels to work. I loved the title of being office manager. It was only when renewing some insurance cover for our home a short time after leaving work that the realisation came. The person on the other end of the phone asked about Alan's employment and then about mine. When they asked what my occupation was, I mumbled, "Housewife!" When I put the phone down at the end of the call I sat on the bottom of the stairs and sobbed.

I had fallen into a trap; I am so grateful to God for the revelation He brought. I was living with the world's equation for identity and I hadn't realised it. The world's equation is that I would get my self-worth from my performance, along with other people's opinions. God was teaching me!

My true identity is what He says about me, plus my believing what He says about me. Events over the following years all brought about my ability to walk in my true identity.

Alan was employed in the construction industry which was going through a major recession. Laying down my career coincided with this time of recession. Most of Alan's colleagues were laid off work but Alan retained his job on a lower wage. The following years were lean but we always had everything that we needed. Sometimes I would travel in the car and minister only to be given a pot plant as a thank you, which I received with the love it was given, but I would be earnestly praying for fuel to put in the car to get me there and back!

We learnt about trusting God for everything, not just spiritual things but practical and physical things. As a family we became well equipped for such a style of living.

I recall during this lean period one of my nieces was getting married and it was going to be a smart wedding. I was browsing in a charity shop and picked up the most magnificent blue coloured two-piece suit in my size. When I looked at the make it was a designer label and it was less than £5. I went off to the wedding looking like someone off the catwalk. I can recall event after event where time and again just the perfect thing would happen at the perfect time. We were living in the provision and favour of God. It was building faith all the time. Alan and I were learning, along with our children, to trust God implicitly.

The second time that I saw miraculous physical healing was when I stepped out in faith regarding Charlotte.

When she was 14 years old she came back from school with a very nasty sore eye. She went up to her bedroom not wanting to talk. I recognised that it was a stye, as I used to get these when I was her age. I prayed internally, not out loud, asking God to heal her and not just to heal the stye but to break any pattern of recurring styes that she may have inherited from me. She eventually came out of her bedroom and asked if I could ring the doctor and see if we could get an appointment for her. We managed to see the doctor immediately. He was very good but told her that, unfortunately, it would get much worse before it got better and that the eye may become so swollen that it would close completely. She was given antibiotic cream to put on the eye and told that it would probably take a week to get better. Everything inside me wanted to pray for her but I sensed to hold back until she asked, as I believed God wanted to do something with Charlotte through this event.

Once we were home, she went back into her bedroom again, not wanting to talk. I continued to pray from a distance but after a while I went up and asked her if I could do anything; she was weeping. She asked me if I would pray with her. I laid hands on her and simply asked the Lord to heal her eye, remove any swelling and cut off any pattern of recurring styes.

The next morning, Alan and I were downstairs when she emerged from the bedroom squealing, shouting and so overjoyed. Her eye was completely back to normal with no mark or evidence of where this nasty stye had been the night before. We all celebrated God's goodness and the answer to prayer. Faith was building in all of us.

Up to this point I had exercised the gift of healing within the confines of my home and family. My faith was growing all the time, however, and on a number of occasions I saw physical healings when I prayed with people other than family.

Looking back on that first trip to the Ukraine, I recall how even in the little things I could see the provision and care of my Heavenly Father. I had a fear of rats which came from living on a farm as a youngster. In 1969, when I was a teenager, they had developed the road which passed our farm. Whilst doing the developments, they had knocked down a smallholding and old farm buildings while digging up drains and sewers. This released drain rats into the locality and they all seemed to move to our farm. They became a nightmare for Ruth, Michael and myself. Mice, in my mind, were smaller versions of rats!

Here we were in the Ukraine, staying in accommodation that was being updated and refurbished to become a holiday centre for children affected by the Chernobyl disaster. The nuclear accident occurred on 26th April 1986 at the No.4 reactor in the Chernobyl Nuclear Power Plant, near the city of Pripyat, in the north of the Ukraine. The room we were allocated had no beds so we slept on two single mattresses on the floor, accompanied by mice. During that two-week period, I turned to God asking Him to keep me safe and give me peaceful sleep. Not only was I set free from the fear of mice but also from flying, leaving home and crossing railway lines.

Crossing railway lines, in a vehicle, caused great anxiety inside me.

The farm where I grew up had a railway line running through the land and during my teenage years a vehicle became stuck on a nearby crossing which caused the derailment of a train and killed eleven people. It was a national disaster which left me with a fear of crossing railway tracks. Each day, whilst in the Ukraine, we had to cross over multiple crossings to get from where we were staying to where we were ministering. I surrendered this fear to God and was set free.

We were located at Mayaky, which is just by the Dnestr River. One day, we walked to the river and prayed and prophesied over the river. The other side of the water really drew me. I did not understand what was drawing me but I took photos of it and when I got home, I looked at the map and saw that the small Republic of Moldova lay just a few miles on. I started to pray about this and a passion for Moldova started to rise within me.

My parents used to pass on to us their copy of a Christian magazine and one day, in the early spring of 1996, I was having a coffee at our breakfast bar when I picked up the paper to read. I turned the pages and couldn't believe my eyes. There, in front of me, was a full page about Moldova and the photographs used in the article were very similar to the ones I had taken a few months earlier in the Ukraine. The article was about how a team from a well-known global mission movement, based in Austria, wanted people to volunteer to travel into Moldova later that spring. There was a contact number in Austria and I knew that this was the next step I needed to take. As soon as Alan got home from work, he read the article and said that I must ring them to get more information.

To cut a long story short, within weeks I was flying off to Austria, this time alone, to meet up with the team and then travel on through Austria, Hungary, Romania and into Moldova. The team consisted of people I had never met before, male and female, teens and older but I was the oldest being in my 40s. Again, I was being stretched and challenged.

It took a few days of travelling by mini bus and as we travelled we picked up people along the way who were going to be on the team for two weeks. The first stop was in Oradea, Romania where we picked up two or three youngsters who were around 18 years old. One of these young women was called Lena. Lena and I shared a bench seat in the minibus and we became inseparable during that trip. As we travelled, we chatted. She was like a sponge soaking up things that I had been learning, things God had revealed to me, things about the Holy Spirit. In turn, she was familiar with the culture of Eastern Europe and taught me so much. Her innocence and humour helped carry me through the homesickness, although I cried myself to sleep every single night. I missed Alan and the children so much. Nearly 30 years on, Lena, her husband and children are special friends of ours who we have remained close to.

When we arrived in Moldova, we were joined by Vasile, a very serious young man, who I really grew to respect. There was a maturity and a steadiness about him; he struck me as a wonderful young man of God.

I'm sharing this trip in detail because of something that happened that affected the rest of my life.

The first week we spent near the southern tip of Moldova near to the border with the Ukraine. The second week we spent in the Transnistria district.

During the first week, I struggled with the attitudes of some of the community where we were placed. It was unusual in that culture for a woman to leave her husband at home. I was questioned about why I was wearing a wedding ring. I had no other jewellery on me and my justification for wearing my wedding ring was that it was blessed and exchanged between Alan and I as part of our covenant of marriage. There were other issues about the role of women in ministry that I was being picked up on. It was a very testing time culminating on the last day with a mission event, in a large village, just outside the town.

The team paired up with men from the church to preach and lead worship in the square later in the day. There was no one to pair with Lena, myself and another young girl, Dani. It was suggested that as three women we could go and distribute fliers around the village. We walked around this very poor sprawling village with smouldering bonfires on the side of the roadways. Geese, hens, and chicks wandered in the muddy track that constituted a road. Neighbours were standing or sitting on the roadside passing the time of day. Lena, who can speak many languages including Romanian and Russian (the two languages of Moldova) engaged with a man who was standing by the side of the road. Dani and I simply waited for her.

Whilst waiting, I had a sense that this man was ill, then I sensed that he was seriously ill, terminally ill. Then I sensed that it was his stomach.

I was internally praying in tongues when I heard Lena calling my name to go over to the man. She started to say that he was unwell and I smiled and said that I knew. She said that it was his stomach and again I smiled and said that I knew.

Lena said, "You can't know. You don't speak or understand Russian." I explained that I believed that God had been showing me this through words of knowledge, a gift of the Holy Spirit. The man asked if the English lady would pray for him. I was alarmed because all week I had been so restricted in what I was allowed to do. I asked Lena to double check that this was okay with the man, that a woman could pray for him and lay hands on him. He agreed but he was so tall I could only rest my hand on his shoulder anyway. I know that as I prayed he was healed. I can't prove it but I believe that this had all been orchestrated by God to show me something. There, in a remote village, up to our ears in mud, God moved so powerfully and showed me that He had called me. He showed me that He had anointed me for ministry and no one would stop how He was going to use me. In that holy moment I surrendered any ministry to Him, not my ministry but His ministry. I knew He took me to that place, on that day, in that painful environment of restrictions to commission me. It was a precious day.

Quite a few years after this event, I was back in that same village and town but this time in the role of overseeing, in the nation of Moldova, on behalf of the international ministry I had served in for many years. I went to Moldova many times over the years but only once back to this place.

I recognised the village as we drove through on our way to the town. I was a different woman the second time round, secure in the call of God on my life. I then questioned would God really take me back to the same town? To the same church? He would and He did. It was so precious as, this time, I was greeted and welcomed with love. I was recognised and received. This time I was able to minister freely. It was such a healing visit and caused me to praise God all the more for His attention to detail. I was learning more and more about the intentionality of God.

I want to share something else with you about Moldova before I move on. After the 1995 pioneering trip into the Ukraine, and the mission trip into Moldova in 1996, I was asked by the ministry to accompany another leader there. The ministry had an invitation to be interviewed by one of the Pentecostal Bishops in Chisinau, in Moldova, and depending on the outcome of that visit, to start pioneering new groups in that nation.

The bishop had said that he would send his secretary to meet us at the airport with a vehicle to transport us back to the accommodation where we would be staying. We came through all the airport checks and we were looking for someone who would be holding a card with our names on.

Imagine my delight when I saw Vasile standing there with the card. We hugged one another, much to the other leader's amazement.

I had not known that Vasile, who had been on the mission team in Moldova, was also the bishop's secretary. He had no idea that one of the women he was meeting at the airport was going to be me.

He already knew me and was enthusiastically sharing with the bishop about knowing me. This definitely was another of those special connections God makes. It further demonstrated to me the fine details that God can weave together in our lives. On the many visits I went to Moldova, Vasile was a great blessing and became a precious friend. He married and then emigrated with his family to America living near Seattle. Once, when I was in Seattle, I was able to spend a short time with him but then we lost touch. However, through the positive use of social media I have recently re-connected with him and his family. I am delighted that they are strong in their faith and serving God's purposes where they now live.

I gave a part of my heart to Moldova. It's been a few years since I handed over the oversight of that nation on behalf of the ministry but I have never stopped loving the people. You can't pour yourself into something and then just walk away. So many wonderful things happened whilst ministering in that nation that were life and character shaping. I grew familiar with the bishops, pastors and leaders in that beautiful country, developing deep relationships and trust. I worked alongside some wonderful people who were a great inspiration to me.

Marina was one Moldovan lady that I had a close working relationship with in the ministry. She had not long become a Christian and had a daughter who was an excellent interpreter. She had invited her mother to a ministry event in her home town and I was drawn to her right from the start. It was so good to see her grow and develop over the years into an excellent leader.

I shared many experiences with that precious family who are still friends today. I developed a great relationship with one of the churches in the capital city of Chisinau, where I loved to join them in worship, feeling welcomed and very much at home there.

From the time when I prayed with the Russian man in the village in the south of Moldova, I went on every trip to Eastern Europe with the expectation of seeing physical healing. Over the years, I had the privilege of praying with a number of people for healing whilst ministering in Moldova.

One occasion that really blessed me, but also taught me something important, was when I was ministering in the North West of Moldova in an extremely poor village. I was there establishing groups on behalf of the international ministry, developing relationships, teaching leadership to potential group leaders and appointing leaders.

One of the leaders asked me to pray for her son who was around eight years of age and had been born with a problem in one of his legs. From my understanding, this disability had been caused by lack of medical assistance when he was being born. It had left him with a leg that was not growing or developing correctly.

It caused him to limp acutely and was preventing him from a normal physically active life. She asked if I would pray for him whilst I was praying for her needs. I did!

At the end of the day, the lady I was travelling with and I were invited to join the leaders of the ministry group and the pastor of the church for some refreshments in the church's basement.

We were blessed by this food and after we had eaten, the pastor asked if we could all pray together. In the meantime, a boy had arrived and I quickly realised this was the boy I had prayed for, with his mother, earlier. The pastor asked if we could link hands and pray in a circle. I reached for the hand next to me which was this young boy. I don't speak either Romanian or Moldovan so we all prayed at the same time in our native language. I prayed for healing for the boy in the name of Jesus and for his leg to become what God had designed originally.

We returned to our overnight accommodation in the capital city where we were being hosted by the Pentecostal Union. The next morning, one of the bishops called me into his office and explained he had received a phone call from the pastor of the church we had been at the day before.

The pastor had told him that the boy's mother had spoken to him because that evening, and throughout the night, the boy had started to get a lot of discomfort in his leg. What he described sounded like intense pins and needles. He had told his mother that it had started when I had held his hand when we were praying at the church.

The pastor told the bishop that overnight the boy's leg had grown and become normal like his good leg. I was so excited, amazed, yet challenged so deeply by this event.

A year later, I was back in Moldova and again met with the mother. I immediately asked how her son was. For me this was a big deal, however, she was very casual about it saying simply he was well; God had healed him but that was what we had prayed for. It hit the spot with me. It challenged me.

What had I been expecting when I had prayed for him? Was I really expecting God to heal Him? If so, why was it such a big deal? Another massive learning and growing curve for me. What are my expectations of God?

Around this time, I was also invited to minister in Romania by a pastor from Petrosani in the Transylvanian Mountains. This was not with the ministry I was serving with. The invitation had come through a connection from another of the young men who had been on the initial mission trip to Moldova. The pastor of a church in Romania needed a lady to do some ministry with women in his church and he didn't know who to ask. It was interesting that despite the pain and restrictions I had experienced during that time of the first trip to Moldova, the young men and women I had travelled with had really appreciated the things I shared with them as we travelled. This young man had recommended me to the pastor and so it was agreed that I would go to Romania for this purpose.

The pastor linked me with a lady and gentleman from the UK who I hadn't met before. The lady, Melanie, had a heart for mission and needed a travel companion. The gentleman, Alex, was a businessman who had donated money to humanitarian work in both Romania and Hungary and wanted to see first-hand how the money was being used.

Prior to our first time of travelling together to Romania, the pastor of a church in Leamington Spa had prayed with me. He said that he believed I would go to Romania with one name but return known by another.

It sounded strange but I held this word privately to see what would happen. Whilst at the church in Petrosani, ministering to the women, the pastor sat at the back of the building watching me and listening. At the end of the ministry time he asked his grandson to translate something important he wanted to share with me. He said that whilst I had been ministering, God had shown him that I was like Elizabeth, the mother of John the Baptist. She had given birth to a child filled with the Holy Spirit (Luke 1:15).

The pastor said to me, "You will have many spiritual children and they will be filled with the Holy Spirit. You are known as Elizabeth, the spiritual mother of many." I was once again amazed. My birth name is Elizabeth Anne. I use both names but am widely and generally known as Anne. This, again, showed me God's interest in the most finite details of my life, my name.

Over a few years, after that trip to Romania, I travelled with Melanie and Alex into Hungary.

It was primarily to support a community located on the north east side of Hungary with aid but whenever we travelled into Hungary we would do teaching and ministry with the people there. All the time I was growing and learning, being exposed to a variety of ministry situations. I was growing in faith through experience.

In preparing the material for this book, I read back through my journals and diaries and noted some insights, prophetic words and pictures I received during the 1990s.

One that really caught my attention was that I had noted on 24th January, 1996 that while I was worshipping, God had shown me the map of the world and drawn my attention to certain continents or nations. Firstly, the UK, then Europe, then South America, then Africa, India and, finally, the other nations.

I had a real sense of an unfolding of a calling to these specific nations in the order that I was shown. I believed that this would happen through the ministry I was serving in; however, I will share more about this in the final chapter.

It was autumn 1999 and, at home, Philip had completed his degree at university and was ready to commit to his long-term girlfriend, Emma, in marriage. We were joyfully planning for their wedding which was to be in May 2000. We had gone to Cambridge for the day to continue the planning for Philip and Emma's wedding when I became unwell, feeling most uncomfortable when I breathed in or out.

On getting home I rang for advice from NHS and they sent an ambulance. I was admitted to hospital with a pulmonary embolism. After a few days in hospital, I was discharged and given blood thinners and just got on with life.

Soon afterwards, I noticed some lumps on my skull within my hair line. After a few more lumps started to appear, I went to my GP who referred me to hospital. I saw a skin specialist who examined them and took a biopsy from one of them. I was given an appointment to return to the same clinic in three weeks.

I duly arrived at the clinic and saw the consultant who said it was nothing to worry about. The GP had carried out blood tests already and all were normal. She said that no cause was identified and may have been sparked off by the clot or a type of immune reaction to the short-term warfarin that I had been on. The reaction could last years and it was often not responsive to treatment. She wrote a few statements on a piece of scrap paper and gave it to me; I still have that piece of paper today! She called it annular erythema. When I questioned her about this, she said it meant a ringlike redness but I needed to forget about them and they would just go away. That is exactly what I did...or tried to.

I was developing so many strong friendships through ministry. I was being surrounded by mature Christians who influenced my life. It was around this time that I met a lovely girl, Tina, when preaching at a church in North Lancashire. It was amazing how this young teenager and I connected though our strong friendship developed later.

Another key event happened at the end of 1999, when tv channel ITV was planning its morning service live from Stafford Castle, which was being organised by Churches Together. I was asked if I would anchor the service and I was honoured to.

It was a beautiful interdenominational act of worship and at the end of the recording we were invited to join the Anglia TV crew for lunch at a local restaurant. During lunch, a number of the production team came and spoke to me about the ease with which I anchored the programme, the clarity and projection of my voice and other very affirming and positive comments.

Soon after, I was approached by Anglia TV, who were the company responsible for producing the Sunday Morning Service at that time, and they asked if I would be interested in becoming the anchor for their new look Sunday Morning Services that were due to be aired in the new year.

I was quite taken aback but extremely honoured, and I said, "Yes." I had just stepped down from area leadership in the international ministry where I had served first as a local leader and then for two years as an area leader covering the South Midlands. The travel had drained me and whilst I loved it and would happily have carried on, the other leaders felt that in light of the recent blood clots I should step down from leadership, which I did. The invitation from Anglia TV came at this time and I felt that this was God opening a new door.

I travelled with a friend to East Anglia to record the first two programmes that were going to be the new series.

I was in my element! I loved it — and so did the crew! They didn't need to do retakes and, again, they were so affirming. I believed that an enormous door of opportunity for sharing Jesus with the nation, via television, was opening and I was ready to walk through it. As this was all happening in the late autumn of 1999, when I wrote our Christmas cards that year, I added a paragraph in the cards to inform our family and friends that if they couldn't watch the programme on the Sunday morning (starting in January) then to set their videos to record. They would have a surprise when they saw who was anchoring the programme.

As part of my preparation for this new opportunity, I had spoken at length with my past minister, Derek. He had been instrumental in my understanding of the Holy Spirit and my call to preach. I ran everything past him as to what I wanted to share as I anchored the programmes. We talked about the importance of naming Jesus as opposed to simply referring to God. I say this because, yes, Jesus is God but when people talk about God, they may not necessarily be referring to Father God, as revealed through Jesus Christ. He seemed surprised that I was being given such a responsible role, but was cheering me on. I was naively unaware what this was all about.

I can only say that when the telephone rang, just before the programmes were schedule to be aired, the presence and grace of God completely enfolded me. The voice on the other end was extremely apologetic saying all sorts of nice things but, actually, saying that they weren't going to air the programmes and that they were going to proceed in a different way. They were so apologetic but told me they wouldn't be using me in the future.

As I put down the telephone and walked slowly back into the lounge to share the news with Alan, I had a picture come very clearly in my spirit imagination. It was of a make-up bag full of various items. I saw, in my mind, the zip being opened and the various items being handled by God's hand and then, very gently, closed again by His hand. Within that brief split second, I sensed God had allowed this all to happen just to see what my reaction to these events would be. It was about obedience and a surrendered life so it was all okay.

I was able to smile and let it all just fall away, knowing that He had just closed a door firmly and that I was to simply move on under His guidance with the door He was about to open.

We moved into the Millennium knowing that God was preparing something for me and I had a sense of new beginnings, which was very exciting. It wasn't long before I took a couple of phone calls from members of the national team from the international ministry that I had been serving under. It was during these two calls that God showed me that He was preparing a way for me to serve on the national leadership team in Great Britain.

Then, in April 2000, I received an official letter from the president of the ministry in Great Britain, asking if I would consider joining the national team. I knew that this was what God really had planned for me and I was delighted and honoured to say, "Yes!"

We celebrated the marriage of our son, Philip, to Emma, on 6th May 2000, and although the lumps on my head were hidden by hair and hat they weren't reducing, in fact, they were increasing in size and number!

I knew that God was going to give me the strength to just rely on the thermals of His Spirit and, like the eagles, I would soar.

Chapter Five
The Promise

As 2000 was about to become 2001, I asked God for a word for the new year. I don't recall exactly what that word was but I know it was to do with faith. For me, every conference, Christian event and even many Sunday services the theme was faith.

Alan and I received so much teaching on faith in the spring of 2001, and I recall a number of times we looked at one another as the preacher would speak from Romans 4, especially from verse 13, which has the heading 'The Promise Granted Through Faith' in my New King James Version of the Bible. I underlined in my Bible a couple of verses in this passage

> "....God, who gives life to the dead and calls those things which do not exist as though they did; ...he did not waver at the promise of God through unbelief, but was strengthened in faith, giving glory to God."

Romans 4:17-20 (NKJV)

Abraham's faith was that God would fulfil His promises based on his belief that God was able to do that which He had spoken. In Romans 4:17 we read that Abraham believed in God. He was not just giving mental assent but was prepared to put complete and utter trust in what God said, and this should be a fundamental truth for us.

Also, from Hebrews 11:1-3:

"Now faith is the substance [or realisation] of things hoped for, the evidence of [or confidence in] things not seen."

Hebrews 11:1-3 (NKJV)

The words in brackets are added by me.

This passage shows me that in order to exercise faith, I need to act on things that I don't yet have the evidence of, or even understand, but that I believe in. In daily life, we all exercise faith without thinking; for example, when switching on a light. I have no idea how it all works but I believe that when I flick the switch, the light will come on; that is exercising faith.

Faith in God is basically acting like God is telling the truth. Faith occurs when we stop trying to do something by our own efforts and trust someone else to do it for us. Faith is the exact opposite of trusting ourselves. This is why God decided that faith would be the way which we could obtain salvation; that it might be of grace, which is an entirely free gift of God, and not dependent on any effort of our own.

Faith enables us to believe and receive all God has for us who believe. By faith we walk in the fullness of the gifts and power of the Spirit. I learnt that faith believes absolutely in the promises of God, the divine inspiration of the Bible and uses God's promises in dealing with issues – personal or for others. Walking by faith is not just for the bold acts of power in the Holy Spirit but also for everyday interactions. Faith is to be expressed through actions and not an idea separate from real life issues.

I had participated in the ministry's spring national conference in early March 2001. Under the spotlights of the platform someone had noticed the lumps, which were no longer confined to my hair line but had spread to my forehead and the side of my head. They said that I ought to go to see a doctor. I too was starting to think I ought to go back to the doctor but I was due to go to Hungary with Melanie and Alex so I decided to leave it until I returned.

It was now obvious to anyone who saw me that I had lesions on my head. Some on the side of my head were so large that my glasses didn't sit properly on my face. Mostly people were kind and never referred to them but travelling and spending so much time that week in Hungary with Melanie, I did talk to her about them.

I wasn't anxious at all. I had the most precious gift in my life, another tool in the tool belt. It's a gift available to everyone who puts their trust in Jesus. It's the gift of peace of heart and mind:

"... *in Me you may have peace."*

John 16:33 (NKJV)

and John 14:27 where Jesus says:

"Peace I leave with you, My peace I give to you; not as the world gives do I give to you. Let not your heart be troubled, neither let it be afraid."

John 14:27 (NKJV)

I had the peace of God which has gone on to fill my life. I recorded in my prayer journal:

"Sat 31st March, 2001. In Hungary the last day of the mission trip. Last night I had a peaceful dream during which someone told me I was very sick. I believe the dream has been given to me to prepare my heart."

I recall this so clearly. Melanie and I were in our bedroom getting ready to go out for the evening in Budapest. She was in the bathroom, putting on her make up, with the door open to the bedroom where I was sitting. I asked her what she thought about the lumps on my face and head.

I asked her, "Do you think it might be cancer?" It went very quiet and she stopped what she was doing and suggested that we prayed together there and then, and that I make an appointment with my doctor as soon as I got home. She didn't answer my question but I knew she thought it was serious. I recorded in my diary: "A thoughtful day!"

I went home and saw my doctor on Monday 2nd April. I was referred back to the same specialist I had seen in 1999.

One of the things I had learnt during the past decade was that even though I had seen miracles of healing, a miraculous healing is not something we can assume. I had lost a number of precious family and friends to cancer despite much prayer and exercising of faith.

I had learnt that there is no formula to healing. We can view death as a failure because we feel the searing loss of a loved one, or we can see how God can be equally present in the death of one of His children.

I had experienced this privilege when being at the side of one of my uncles, who I loved dearly, as he passed away. Before he stopped breathing, it was the most beautiful moment. There was such a sense of peace and God's presence in the room. A Macmillan nurse had stayed overnight with me and when I recognised my uncle had stopped breathing, I turned to the nurse and saw she was kneeling on the floor weeping. She said she had never experienced anything like it. She described how she saw both my uncle and I enveloped in a sort of mist. She recognised the holiness of the moment and got on her knees. I had not felt or seen anything myself, other than this sense of peace and God's presence in the room. The nurse later connected with me outside of her work situation and made a commitment to Jesus Christ.

I received an appointment to see the skin consultant the following week, on Monday 9th April, which was the start of Holy Week. She took a biopsy from one of the lumps on the top of my skull and I asked her if she thought it might be cancer. Her reply was, "I can confidently say that you have cancer, but what this biopsy will tell us is what sort of cancer."

To face the full impact of the word 'cancer' was tough and more so because Alan was away from home, due to work commitments, until the Thursday.

I shared with Alan, over the phone, the factual aspect of the appointment, but I didn't want to share with him that I was sensing I was in a very serious situation.

As I have already stated, it was Holy Week and I had planned to take Charlotte to a large retail outlet the next day as a mother/daughter day. Charlotte had taken a year out before going to Loughborough University so was still living at home. As I look back, I see God's hand in this.

Charlotte had her place at university confirmed but it meant she was around for the period of time when I needed her. I hadn't been to this retail outlet before but she had, and we were both looking forward to it. I remember going there and being in a sort of daze. I think it was just a form of shock but there wasn't any fear.

That night I experienced the first night sweat. I was alarmed at just how soaked I was and I wrote in my journal the next day, "During last night I wanted Alan to hold me, not because I was afraid but I felt that his strength would strengthen me."

Two days later, I recorded, "God reminded me today that I am His covenant child." What an identity! I am bound to Him in a loving relationship that nothing can affect. Romans 8:35 reminds us that there is NOTHING that can separate us from the love of God — no illness, not even death. I am held safe in His love and He is a covenant God who cannot break or fail to keep His word. I knew the security of being held steady by God Himself.

I was expecting Alan home late on Thursday evening as his journey was long.

He wasn't home when the phone rang and the lady on the end introduced herself as the consultant I had seen on Monday. She explained that it was coming up to a Bank Holiday weekend and asked me to go to hospital on Tuesday morning when she would share the results of the biopsy. She asked if I could take someone, preferably my husband, with me to the appointment. It was a hard conversation I had with Alan as he arrived home from work that evening.

Philip and Emma were coming to stay for the weekend. I shared with them when they arrived on Good Friday about going to see the GP and the very quick appointment with the consultant following the phone call. I felt a bit emotional as I shared but got strength as we spent time together.

I was to preach on Easter Sunday morning, 15th April 2001, at St John's Church in Stone. I had done a lot of the preparation and I was going to be speaking on lines from 1 Corinthians 15:54-57:

> "O death where is your sting...death is swallowed up in victory...thanks be to God who gives us the victory through our Lord Jesus Christ."

1 Corinthians 15:54-57 (NKJV)

As part of the act of worship, I wanted to share a story about the transformation of a caterpillar to a butterfly, primarily for the children. Often, the simple illustrations seem to be the thing that people grasp best.

Emma is very gifted with drawing, as well as being a qualified children's nursery nurse, so she spent time on the Saturday drawing and colouring illustrations to go along with the caterpillar talk. She was working on the floor in our lounge when she stopped, looked up at me and simply said, "This is a big deal for us, but it isn't a big deal for God." I recorded her exact words in my journal and drew strength from reading and re-reading them over the days and weeks that followed.

I remember well the sense of God's presence on that Easter Sunday morning service as I declared from the pulpit the promises of God. Only my family knew the situation we were in and the giant we were about to face. As I made declarations from that pulpit, the declarations were being heard by the congregation, the powers and principalities of the spirit world and myself, and they strengthened me.

On Tuesday morning, Alan and I travelled to the hospital. We arrived early and I went into one of the toilets and read a text message from a friend who I had shared with. Her message was full of promise and the truth of God's Word. When we went and sat down with the consultant, she shared that I had non-Hodgkin lymphoma, a very serious type of cancer.

I can remember my mouth going dry and what felt like an icy grip round my ankles. It was an ugly feeling and I didn't like it. I recognised it as fear. I was in shock and I was afraid. I recalled from the Bible what John had written in one of his letters, 1 John 4:18:

"There is no fear in love, but perfect love casts out fear."

1 John 4:18 (NKJV)

Our church had been celebrating its 100th Anniversary that weekend with various activities planned. The church and my parents were expecting us, not only join in the festivities but actually to host some of them. I remember just going through the motions whilst inside I was numb.

I read the account of when Jesus was asleep in the boat during the storm Matthew 8:23-26. The contrast between Jesus and the disciples impacted me. Jesus was sleeping through the very same circumstances that were causing the disciples to panic. The disciples could only see the height of the waves and they believed they would be overwhelmed by them. The voices in their heads would be going something like, "You are going to die. You're not going to get through this."

I found myself identifying with the disciples and I realised that I was walking in a similar situation. They were out of control and their very lives were in danger.

In 2 Corinthians 5:7 we are encouraged to walk by faith and not by sight. I knew that I needed to live by faith and not what I could see with my natural eye. I knew I needed to live in alignment to the truth of God's Word and promises, so I turned to the Bible for inspiration to calm those mounting waves. I sought God for His perspective on the situation and was able to draw on a peace that was going to help me through the storm.

I spent the next few days applying all that I had been learning about faith, trust, love and promises. The fear left me! I felt strong enough to deal with whatever needed dealing with on a daily basis. I kept declaring the promises of God over my life.

I recognised I was in a situation where nothing I could do would change it. It didn't matter that I was a much-loved daughter, wife, mother, sister, friend; not one of them could do anything to change this situation. I had to choose to trust God completely because He was the only One who could.

I have had the blessing of a prayer partner, Sue, for about 30 years. I felt that I should go and see her and tell her in person what the consultant had shared with Alan and me. We lived in the same village, and I remember walking to her home and she opening the door and looking at me, searching my face for evidence of what news I would be sharing with her. She then ushered me into her lounge where I shared what I had been told.

I remember being very strong and positive but could see the struggle on her face. She wept as I shared with her. Recently, when praying together, she recalled that day and sent me a few thoughts in an email:

"When you arrived at the front door, you said you wanted to speak with me rather than over the telephone. We went into the sitting room and sat down opposite each other. You then told me of your diagnosis — immediately I started to cry and gave you a hug but you were so calm (I felt guilty that I was unable to control my blubbering and to be strong for you). You then went into a little more detail of what the next stage would be, that it was not good, but you trusted God and whatever His plan was, He would be with you. After you left, I felt numb and prayed to God asking for your healing. A few more tears and then realising your faith was so strong.

He would sustain you through whatever lay ahead, although I personally struggled at that time.

"I was aware that Alan and the family would be going through a lot of emotions, but you were in my upper thoughts. It was only some time later that I realised just how much Alan and the family were affected by it all and needed just as much prayer."

We look back now, and hardly recognise the women we were then, as God has transformed us both through His love for us.

Reading back through my journal over those immediate days there followed a series of daily hospital appointments. Due to his workload, Alan couldn't go to some but Charlotte was able to attend. She was a great support with her strong and steady faith.

I was due to fly to Moldova at the beginning of May and God had given me a clear word. It was a word from Isaiah 45:2:

"I will go before you and will level the mountains..."
Isaiah 45:2 (NIV)

Something I have noted over the years is that when God gives me a message for a nation, or an individual, He has always made a way for me to deliver it.

I had also had a prophetic word given to me by a reliable friend on 19th April, 2001.

It was that I would be used by God to encourage others not to give up but I would pioneer a path of faith. It was a big mountain that I was facing but I would reach over the top. It may at times feel slippery but God would support and strengthen me.

The national leadership of the ministry were a great source of support and encouragement. The individual members were constantly in touch with reminders of God's promises and just expressions of love and affirmation.

Alan and I had booked a week's holiday in Scotland but were thinking that we would need to cancel it. On the morning of Monday 23rd April, I had a number of telephone conversations with various departments at the hospital about appointments. The hospital suggested that we go away for a few days, so we got drove to Fort William.

The next day, we took the gondola ride to the top of Annoch Mor. We walked around the mountain top, had a coffee and then walked to one side of the mountain where we found a soft grassy area and had a picnic. Afterwards, we just lay there in silence, looking up at the sky, only to be disturbed by an eagle when it flew from around the back of the mountain. We both lay watching it and it felt very significant. We simply watched its graceful soaring. It had no frantic activity, it simply stretched out its wings, caught the thermals and rose on them. Suddenly, again from behind the mountain, the eagle was joined by another and we watched the two of them rising and moving in well-orchestrated, well-choreographed harmony.

I knew deep within that God was showing me something really important. It wasn't a lonesome eagle, it had a partner it moved alongside and they were as one. I knew that God was with me, by His Spirit and, in the natural, it was Alan and I together. I knew that God was going to give me the strength to rely only on the thermals of His Spirit and, like the eagles, I would soar.

When we got back to sea level, we drove along Glen Nevis and parked up by the information centre at Ben Nevis, the highest mountain in the UK. We had a good look around and, with my love of maps, I spent ages studying the area. It was then that I had a flashback to when Alan and I had visited Fort William just after Philip was born. I wanted to climb Ben Nevis, but with a baby in a sling and no suitable footwear or clothing, Alan suggested we should return when Philip was older and we were better prepared. Although we both said we would climb the highest mountain in the UK, we had never done it! I reminded Alan and he simply smiled.

I was about to leave the centre when I realised Alan had something in his hand and was heading to the pay desk. He came out with a guide map of how to climb Ben Nevis, the route and history. He simply said, "When you are better, we are going to climb this mountain." I teased him endlessly after that because Alan has never been one to make bold statements like that, nor to spend money on something he wasn't going to use. This simple action meant so much to me. This is faith. Alan had invested in something that, in the natural, seemed impossible but it was to become such a focus over the next twelve months.

I have to say that I had found a strength in God and His promises that meant that I was able to continue to function both with the responsibilities in the ministry and also in our church, home and with the family. I was unsure about what lay ahead, however. I attended regular appointments for tests, scans etc. at the hospital while they investigated how far the cancer had spread. I was also receiving insight and revelations from God about the upcoming ministry trip to Moldova and the two didn't seem compatible — in fact they definitely weren't compatible in the natural.

I was waiting for a date for a CT scan and also an appointment to see the surgeon. I had my flights booked for Moldova for the first two weeks in May and I really believed that I was going to go to take the word that I felt I had been given. I packed my bags in readiness to go, apart from the last minute things, and then I received an appointment for the CT scan which was to be on 1st May. Thankfully, it was before my planned trip.

On the evening of Tuesday 1st May, after having had the CT scan, I went to bed with Alan and fell fast asleep. I awoke in the middle of the night feeling a gentle weight on my head. I thought it must be Alan laying hands on me while I slept. I turned to face his side of the bed only to find him lying with his back to me. I instantly knew this was a manifestation of God. I started to worship Him and felt the bedroom fill with His presence. The weight of the 'hand' on my head remained and I felt warmth go through my whole body. I heard Him as clear as anything. I don't think it was audible but deep and clear in my mind saying, "Anne, this sickness will not lead to your death but it will be a testimony to the nations of My power and Glory".

I continued to worship and savour the moment until I fell into a deep sleep that lasted until morning. I was cocooned in God's love. It was such a revelation of the depth and intimacy of His love for me; He had addressed me by name and made me a promise. The awareness of His love was sculpting my true identity.

I rang one of the other national leaders from the ministry and shared what had happened. I needed the accountability which I am so grateful for as she can confirm to this day the contents of that phone call. I had received a touch from The King (Jesus) — and one touch from The King changes everything. It was quite some months later, when reading through Psalm 118:17, that I felt it affirmed:

"I will not die but live and proclaim what the Lord has done."

Psalm 118:17 (NIV)

And some time later when reading John 11:4:

"This sickness will not end in death. No it is for God's glory so that God's Son may be glorified through it."

John 11:4 (NIV)

When God speaks, it is always in alignment with Scripture. I wrote in my journal, the next day, "I am so aware of a deep peace throughout my body. I'm awake but feel like my inside is asleep or rested. I have less discomfort than I have had for days."

I am the beloved child of the Living God and I can access Him at any time day or night.

Chapter Six
Who am I really?

I attended a meeting with the surgeon who had been appointed to look after me at my local hospital. When he shared that the CT scan had shown nothing alarming it was good news, but he needed to do a lymph gland biopsy. He explained that he was going to be out of the country for the next three weeks and he felt that as things had been left this long, there was no problem in leaving it a bit longer. He said that he was due back on the same day that I was due back from Moldova, so I asked him if he thought I could go. He enthusiastically agreed that I should and when family rang that evening to see how I had got on, I was finishing my packing ready to fly!

While in Moldova, God used me in exercising the gift of miracles. I prayed for a leader who had been diagnosed with a serious prognosis of cancer. I was able to anoint her with oil and, along with other leaders, we laid hands on her and prayed for healing in the name of Jesus. It was on a future trip that I was told she was healed and well. I came home uplifted, knowing that God could do the same for me.

I read from Mark 5:34 and underlined the verse in my Bible and printed it off. It's the story of the woman who touched the hem of Jesus's garment. This woman was cut off from normal life because, in that culture, she was considered to be unclean.

She had spent all her wealth on physicians and her health was deteriorating, so reached out in faith to Jesus by touching the hem of the clothes He was wearing. It was an act of faith.

We read what Jesus said to her:

> *"Daughter, your faith has made you well. Go in peace and be healed of your affliction."*

> **Mark 5:34 (NKJV)**

I received this as a personal word to apply, through prayer, to my situation. I also saw how, at the start of this story, the woman is unknown other than she is unclean. At the end of the story she has her true identity. Jesus addresses her as daughter. I learnt so much about identity during these times.

The lumps and lesions had spread to other parts of my body, including the side of my face, as well as across my scalp and my upper trunk. The non-Hodgkin lymphoma was prominent in my skin. The experts said it was slightly unusual. They asked if I minded them being photographed and used for teaching purposes. I was happy for this to happen.

At times I was very vulnerable emotionally and any hint of death had the effect of making me wobble. Alan was rock solid and, if he suspected a wobble, he would quickly remind me of the night of 1st May. He often reminded me that there were many unfulfilled prophesies over my life that would yet be fulfilled. I couldn't cope with TV medical dramas so they were all switched off.

I did not need to feed on what the world says about this type of cancer, I only needed to hear what God was saying. Alan acted as a buffer between me and anyone, or anything, which brought a negative spin.

He once went to answer the doorbell and, after the person had gone, I heard him go to the bin. I asked him who had been and what had gone in the bin. He said who it was and that they had brought sympathy, talked as if I was already dead and had brought an arrangement of flowers and greenery that looked like a wreath. He wouldn't have it in the house. He was amazing!

Alan took on such a protective role and I needed that because I was still learning to apply all that I had been taught. We have a great biblical example of this as recorded in Luke 8:51, where it describes a life and death situation of a young girl. Jesus only allowed three of His disciples to go into the house, along with the child's mother and father. Jesus wouldn't let anyone with unbelief get near the child. He placed that protective hedge around her and her parents.

I devoured the Word of God and drank in His love, presence and promises. I received so many words from friends across Great Britain and other nations. I was grateful to God for the teaching I was receiving through the ministry, the prayer support and love. I felt that I should not receive the laying on of hands from anyone following the experience I had overnight on 1st May. I believed that God was keeping things so that no-one could boast or claim that they were the one God used. The people God used were unaware of the fact that they were being used as instruments of healing.

I had the gland biopsy on 1ˢᵗ June and a lymph node removed. The surgeon said that it had been a bigger procedure than he had expected. It was very painful! It left me with weakness in my left arm and shoulder, and limited neck movement as well as deep pain. It was a number of years before I was healed of the pain and weakness that came as a result of that procedure. It's an amazing story of healing in its own right that I will share in a later chapter.

Alan and I felt that we were being judged from two directions. Whether this was the case or not I don't know, but it's what we felt. On the one hand, there were Christians who thought that we were in denial; that by trusting God for healing, and not preparing for death, was unrealistic. All they could offer was sympathy. Then there were those Christians who thought that my decision to have treatment was demonstrating a lack of faith. They challenged my decision to have chemotherapy, saying that putting poison into my body was not God's will for my life and showed a lack of trust. If God wanted to heal me, then He would heal me but not with chemotherapy. I received a phone call from a Christian I know, who asked if I had 'unforgiveness' in me as that can cause cancer. I needed to repent so that I could be healed. Needless to say, I found this time stressful.

I recorded in my journal on Friday 15ᵗʰ June that I had an upsetting stressful day with phone calls, and on Sunday 17ᵗʰ June, "Felt a loss of peace for the first time since diagnosis." I was unsettled over whether to pursue treatment or not.

Then Derek, our past minister (the one who had been instrumental in my call to preach), having heard how ill I was, called on me whilst he was visiting the area. He talked and prayed with me and, as the day went by, I felt more settled. I was ready to make the decision. I recorded in my journal that, "I will pursue treatment today, Wednesday 20th June."

The surgeon had spoken about not knowing which consultant to refer me to, but that he had 'found' himself taking lunch with the senior doctor, a consultant haematologist. After sharing my situation with him, and seeking his advice, he was going to refer me to him.

The decision Alan and I made at that point was to trust God for healing through the wisdom and advice of this Consultant Haematologist. We prayed that God would use the consultant as His hands, His will, etc and that if the consultant started to go down a route that was not right for me, that God would cause him to change his mind. Fortunately, we were surrounded by our own children and a number of friends who stood with us in our decision.

It was about ten days later, the beginning of July 2001, that I first met the man who I now refer to as my consultant. He was certainly God's man for the task. I trusted him and we developed a mutual respect for one another. I started a course of chemotherapy, in early July, as an outpatient at the local hospital. The consultant and his team were amazing. The nurses who took my blood were so warm and they enjoyed their work, making us all feel very special and relaxed.

The staff in the haematology day ward who administered the chemotherapy were friendly and yet very professional. I can only speak extremely highly of the care I received. Nearly every time I visited this clinic over a period of 10 years, I was personally seen by my consultant. Sometimes those visits were daily, sometimes weekly or monthly, eventually annually. Whenever I attended that department I felt loved and cared for by all the staff — I felt valued.

In Matthew's Gospel, chapter six, there is a long discourse recorded of Jesus's teaching, and part of that records Jesus explaining the value He places on birds.

"Are you not of more value than they?"

Matthew 6:26 (NKJV)

The value of what Jesus places on me was becoming very real.

On 20th July, 2001, I went with Charlotte and Alan to buy a wig. I had started to lose my hair, my eyebrows and eyelashes quite quickly. I had red marks all over my face, and so I thought I would select a wig that would make me look more attractive. I chose a light coloured, slightly wavy one, which would cover my forehead and sides to detract from the lesions that were visible. I placed a lot of confidence in the wig to transform me. However, when I tried to wear the wig in an attempt to make me look more normal, it made my scalp itch so much it drove me mad. I lost confidence in its ability to help me and I grew to really dislike it.

Very quickly, I decided not to wear the wig, so even if I started out in a morning with it on, most of the time I would take it off before long. I knew that it might be hard for some people to see me like I was but I chose to place my confidence in how God sees me. I learnt that the inner beauty shines out and that the glory of His presence would transform what was seen. I felt so loved by God and my family and friends. I was so peaceful that even when I saw my reflection in the mirror, I was okay with it. I learnt, again, so much about identity through all of this.

It was so amazing how God answered our prayer. There were occasions when my consultant would suggest that at the next visit he would do such and such. If I did not witness to that and pondered on it, talked it through with Alan and prayed about it, the next time the consultant would say something along the lines of, "I had thought to do that, but actually I will do this." I constantly saw God in all the treatment, directing, overseeing and upholding.

I recorded in my journal, on 1st August, 2001, that I declared in prayer, using part of Mark 16:18:

"If they drink anything deadly it will by no means hurt them..."

Mark 16:18 (NKJV)

Although I was going to have this mixture of cytotoxic drugs into my veins, it would do me no long-term harm but would be used by God to destroy the cells that needed destroying. I had a surprising but very thought-provoking conversation with the nurse, who administered the first bout of chemotherapy in the clinic.

She said something along the lines of how some of her patients knew they were dying and had the opportunity to do, and say, things while they could. She added, "The rest of us carry on as if we won't ever die."

As I am writing, I am reading through my journal where I recorded the days of the early treatment. I really didn't like the night sweats. I need to share that there were hard times, emotional times, physically painful times and fun times but, through it all, I experienced peace and joy and an overwhelming sense of the presence of God.

In Psalm 29:11 it says,

> "The Lord will give strength to His people; the Lord will bless His people with peace."
> **Psalm 29:11 (NKJV)**

Our circumstances can evoke in us a sense of weakness and anxiety but because of belonging to God, we can enjoy a sense of strength and peace. That is certainly my experience. I did have times of needing assurance; I was only too aware of how poorly I was.

I have also been surprised at the fact that I was still preaching, still functioning in ministry leadership, still editing and putting together the ministry's magazine; still speaking at conferences and then, to our delight, Charlotte's boyfriend, Austin, asked us if he could ask Charlotte to marry him!

After a couple of months of chemotherapy I noticed a change in my voice. It became wobbly and deeper.

I struggled with this because my voice is not just a means of sharing the gospel but also for singing. I love to worship with singing.

I'd received another bout of treatment, the day before 11th September, 2001, and was resting on the sofa when Charlotte ran downstairs and asked if she could put the television on as there was something going on in the USA. It was the destruction of the Twin Towers and what has become known as 9/11. As we watched it together unfolding in front of our eyes, I was so aware of the fragility of life and that the hundreds of people caught up in this had no idea, when they left for work that morning, how the day would unfold. I recalled what the chemotherapy nurse had said that first time, "Most people get up in a morning, thinking they have years of life ahead of them, not knowing they will die before the end of the day."

On a day when I felt fear trying to come in to my mind and heart, I had to purposely choose to reject the fear. I found a note in my Bible dated 13th September, 2001 and it was Psalm 56. It says it is a prayer for God's help when the Psalmist's life is threatened:

"Whenever I am afraid, I will trust in You. In God (I will praise His word) In God I have put my trust; I will not fear."

Psalm 56:3-4 (NKJV)

I learnt that to focus on Jesus took my focus off the things that sought to unsettle me.

I used extensive periods of worshipping alongside worship songs to help me do that even on days when I didn't feel like it. In fact, on those days I recognised it was more important to do so, and soon I would be abandoned to God in worship. I actually found that by taking a certain physical stance in my lounge as I worshipped was helpful. Now I know that God is not restricted to a particular place but it helped me, and continues to help me, to imagine Him in a corner of the room. I would stand, bow and kneel, all privately towards that corner, whilst visualising my fears, with my circumstances and my struggles being located behind me. That way, I was choosing to turn my back on the things that unsettled me, and put my focus wholly on Jesus. As I was doing so, I was declaring my love, my gratitude, expressing wonder at His nature and all He has done for me. I found that the things that unsettled me, paled into insignificance in the light of who He is. That is another reason I love that little chorus:

"Turn your eyes upon Jesus, look full in His wonderful face, and the things of earth will grow strangely dim in the light of His glory and grace."

Sometimes, I still do this. I find the physical stance helps me to choose where my focus is.

Towards the end of September 2001, I was speaking at a conference in East Anglia. I asked the ministry team if they would pray with me at the end, especially about my voice. They did and the next day my voice was restored back to normal! I've had no further problems with my voice from that day.

At the end of the month, Charlotte left for Loughborough University and I really missed her presence in the home both, spiritually and physically. I am blessed with so many friends and always one of them, or my sister Ruth, was available to go with me to appointments or procedures whilst Alan was at work. There was always someone with flesh on bones to stand alongside, for which I am so grateful to God.

I started to get aches, swelling and itchiness in my veins from having so many needles inserted. My consultant told me it was phlebitis and it may cause a delay with continuing the treatment. It was a Friday and I was due to have the next dose of treatment on the Monday. I was speaking at a Christian event in Northampton that same night and my arms ached as I drove there. At the end of the ministry time I asked the leadership for prayer and especially for the phlebitis to go. They prayed and the aches, itchiness and swelling went and it never came back. I was able to have the treatment on the Monday with no difficulties. Future chemotherapy treatment on my hands never even left a bruising of the veins.

I had shared with a leader in the ministry, who was a qualified nurse, the specific drug details of the chemotherapy that I was on for the nine months. Her comment was that it was a very strong course and that it was amazing I was still able to function with all my responsibilities whilst receiving such treatment. This was verified in January 2002 when attending a leadership conference in Barcelona, Spain.

Staying in the same hotel were some medics from Médecins Sans Frontiers. They were intrigued by what the international ministry was about and where we were from. One of our ladies was sharing about her faith and referred to me. She called me into the conversation and I shared about the diagnosis and how God had spoken to me. The man asked me what form of chemotherapy I was on, so I showed him the card that I had to carry with me, which recorded the mix and level of the drugs. His eyes widened as he read the card and said something along the lines of, it was amazing that I was on those levels of drugs and functioning as normal. One of the verses that I claimed for my situation, as I needed to be physically strong to fulfil my responsibilities, was Isaiah 41:10:

> *"Fear not, for I am with you. Be not dismayed for I am your God. I will strengthen you, Yes, I will help you, I will uphold you with my righteous right hand."*

Isaiah 41:10 (NKJV)

I know this is a verse that I have taken out of its original context but because it stood out to me as I was reading my Bible, I took hold of this passage to apply to my situation.

I thank God that I had learnt the power of declaration. In the passage from the Bible in Isaiah 44:24-28 it shows so clearly the formative power of the spoken word. I recalled 1986 when the power of the Holy Spirit came on me along with the prophetic words I was given.

I was reading the opening chapters of Genesis, and noted for the first time something that I hadn't noted before in this well-known sentence. God spoke — and it was...as simple as that. God said, "Let there be..." and it was. This tied in so much with the passage on faith and the power of declaration from Romans 4:17:

> "God, who gives life to the dead and calls those things which do not exist as though they did..."

Romans 4:17 (NKJV)

It's a form of prayer that I regularly use. We have authority through the death and resurrection of Jesus Christ and so every day I would declare, over my body, that any rogue cells must die, my blood count needed to line up with God's original design for my body and so on. I would declare, "Things may look like this in the natural but God, I declare that...whatever."

Jesus earned that authority and has delegated it to us, His body here on earth. This is not name it and claim it but applying the authority to declare what God has already said.

I love the account recorded in Matthew 8:5-13, where the great faith of the Roman Centurion is shown, and the authority of Jesus is portrayed. Jesus said that He would go to the Roman official's home and that He would restore the Centurion's servant. The Centurion took Jesus at His word; in fact, he believed that Jesus could heal the servant simply by speaking the word, through declaration, and not needing to visit his home.

As we hear the Word, do we accept it? Believe it? Take Him at His word? The Centurion took Jesus at His word. Jesus didn't physically go but when the Roman official went back home, he found the servant healed. I kept feeding my mind with such examples from the Bible, and I continue to do this to this very day. Transforming faith changes us and moulds us into His image. I typed up passages from the Bible and put them around the house where I would see them. I still have a few on display in my study such as Philippians 4:6-7:

"Be anxious for nothing, but in everything by prayer and supplication, with thanksgiving, let your requests be made known to God; and the peace of God, which surpasses all understanding, will guard your hearts and minds through Christ Jesus."

Philippians 4:6-7 (NKJV)

Here, the word 'surpasses' means to rise above; so the peace of God, which is above my human understanding, is going to keep my thoughts, my mind and my heart in that beautiful state of peace. Of course, we are human and there are things that create anxiety but growing in faith and trust, and believing that God will do what He has said He will do, will get us to a place where we are anxious for nothing. This is part of this story: how I grew and continue to grow to that place of total peace.

The peace that I experienced is an important part of the story because I was able to eat, sleep and exercise very well during the investigations and treatment.

This contributed significantly to how my body dealt with the invasive treatment.

The gift of peace is not emphasised enough in my opinion. It is a gift given by Jesus to those who believe. In John 14:27 it states,

> "Peace I leave with you, My peace I give to you; not as the world gives do I give to you. Let not your heart be troubled, neither let it be afraid."

John 14:27 (NKJV)

The word for peace used in the original text is "eirene" and it means a state of rest, quietness and calmness. It's an absence of strife and gives tranquillity. It generally denotes a perfect well-being. What a gift! Why wouldn't everyone want and apply this gift?

I have already shared about my love of singing. I love to worship through song. I had learnt years beforehand to 'sing in the Spirit', that is to sing in tongues to my own made-up tunes and worship. Worship is something that many are better qualified to share about. However, I know that worship is a lifestyle, it certainly is not just what we do for an hour on a Sunday. It is not just singing hymns or songs. It is an expression of gratitude directed to God, Father, Son and Holy Spirit: something from deep within my heart and spirit acknowledging who He is. I love to do just that. I often would sing my own words but always when I was on my own.

I was preparing a sermon I was going to preach, and the passage I was led to were two verses from Jeremiah 17:7-8:

"Blessed is the man who trusts in the Lord and whose hope is the Lord. For he shall be like a tree planted by the waters, which spreads out its roots by the river, and will not fear when heat comes; but its leaf will be green, and will not be anxious in the year of the drought, nor will cease from yielding fruit."

Jeremiah 17:7-8 (NKJV)

I knew as I read this short passage that this described me. I saw in my mind this tree with roots going down deep, searching out, and drawing up the abundance of water from an underground river, flourishing and fruitful. I saw the scorching sun and the absence of rain. I sensed this was not going to be a short period of time but that "the year of the drought" spoke of a long period. As I have said earlier, God often speaks to me through a sensing. I think at this point I knew that this illness wasn't going to be over quickly.

I started to prepare myself mentally for the long haul. I started to think a lot about inheritance. My parents were tenant farmers, they didn't own their own land. We had a comfortable life but they had to work very hard to make ends meet. They had to be creative in their farming methods and diversify to support their income from traditional farming. We had no family silver. In material terms we had no inheritance.

However, my siblings and I had the best inheritance because we were brought up in a Christian home with praying parents.

Alan and I had no material generational inheritance to pass on to our children but when Philip and Charlotte left home for university, and to get married, we gave them both the key to our house and said that they had unlimited unconditional access to the home and all its contents. If they were ever travelling in the vicinity, whether we were home or not, they could come in and help themselves to whatever was in the fridge, or cupboards, because this was part of their inheritance. You see, God was showing me that as His child I had access to all that He is and has. I have unlimited access to His presence, His gifts, His love, His nature. I don't have to go through another person or ritual, I am the beloved child of the Living God and I can access Him at any time, day or night. As these truths were revealed into my very being, drip by drip, I was receiving revelation about who I really am.

I was reading 'A Heart Ablaze' by John Bevere and in one chapter he refers to the greatness and power of God's glory seen in creation:

"He has made the earth by His power. He has established the world by His wisdom."

Jeremiah 10:12 (NKJV)

That reference is, to the inhabited world, the substance. He proceeds to write about cells, the building blocks of the human body, plants, animals and every other living thing. He writes about the millions of cells in our body, a vast variety of which He has designated to grow, multiply and eventually die, right on schedule. He explains in great detail how the cells are made up of different particles and throws out the question, "What force holds its energetic particles together? It's known scientifically as atomic energy but this is a term to describe something that cannot be explained scientifically."

Hebrews 1:3 says,

"God is upholding all things by the word of His power."

Hebrews 1:3 (NKJV)

Colossians 1:17 says,

"He holds all creation together."

Colossians 1:17 (NLT)

Therefore, each time I made a declaration about my healing, I was speaking to the cells in my body and commanding them to grow, multiply and die on the schedule as determined by my Creator and Loving Heavenly Father, God.

I soon found out that my consultant was a keen hill and mountain walker, and we used to talk about different parts of the UK and overseas which were good for walking. I shared with him that Alan and I wanted to climb Ben Nevis as soon as I was well enough. He encouraged me throughout the months of treatment and suggested when he thought I would be strong enough to do it.

I had well-meaning people who would tell me that my immune system would always be compromised, that I wouldn't ever have a normal functioning life, that I'd lack energy, lack strength etc. I had to banish such thoughts. There was a steep slope in the car park that I always used to park in when I went shopping in the town. I used to run up this slope, thinking nothing of it, until I was ill and hadn't the strength. At this point, I set myself the goal of being strong and well enough to be able to run up it once I had finished the treatment — then I would start to prepare for Ben Nevis!

Another passage from the Bible that God laid on my heart was from the book of Daniel where the three friends of Daniel were thrown into the furnace. Someone was preaching on this and I felt the Holy Spirit impress on my heart something to hold on to. In the story, the King has made a decree that everyone should bow down and worship a golden image. There were some young Jewish men who refused to worship anyone or anything other than their God, the God revealed to them over the years. The King ordered that these three young men should be thrown into a fiery furnace that would be heated up seven times hotter than usual. It was so hot that it killed the King's men whose job it was to throw them in! After the young men had been thrown in, the King looked at the three friends but actually saw four, one like the Son of God walking in the midst of the fire, and none of them were hurt.

The friends were brought out of the furnace, and it says in Daniel 3:27:

> *"...they saw these men on whose bodies the fire had no power; the hair of their head was not singed nor were their garments affected, and the smell of fire was not on them."*

Daniel 3:27 (NKJV)

I knew that Jesus, who was with them in the furnace, was with me too. I wouldn't even smell of the smoke; in other words, there would be no after-effects. I wouldn't have a compromised immune system, I wouldn't be weak and I wouldn't lack energy. I received that promise for myself. People who have ministered alongside me, over recent years, have given me the loving nickname 'Duracell Bunny' who, as a UK commercial claimed, has batteries that keep going beyond normal expectations!

At times throughout the investigations and treatment, I had to really choose my response to the things that I was being told. I had to fix my thoughts. I had to think the right thoughts.

The word "think" as used in Philippians 4:8: "...think about such things" means to compute, or think in a calculated way, to come to a conclusion, to reckon, to count, to consider. I had to come to the right conclusion with my thoughts. I didn't fix my thoughts on the medical reports — I listened to them but I fixed my thoughts on the promises and Word of God. His word to me that night was that this sickness was not unto death but for the glory of God.

If I started to have thoughts that were taking me to the wrong conclusion, I simply had to replace it with a different thought.

I would turn to the passages in the Bible that encouraged me. In fact, I would often type up a sheet of A4 paper, with a number of Bible verses that related to a topic, and I would keep that sheet of paper in my Bible. If I started to sense any anxiety, or any loss of peace, I would just read through a number of verses that would remind me of what God says. For example, Colossians 3:2 says,

"Set your mind on things above, not on things on the earth."

Colossians 3:2 (NKJV)

And Isaiah 26:3-4,

"You will keep him in perfect peace, whose mind is stayed on You, because he trusts in You. Trust in the Lord forever, for in YAH, the Lord is everlasting strength."

Isaiah 26:3-4 (NKJV)

To have your mind 'stayed' on Him means to be upheld in thought by Him and to be established in Him, His truth, His promises and His Word. The perfect peace it refers to in this passage is the word shalom, which includes health, happiness and well-being.

The word 'mind' in this passage is not the usual Hebrew word used for mind but it refers to our creative imagination, the seat of plans and ideas, which need to be firmly founded on God. It's only then that we will enjoy shalom and all that it implies. I can assure you, I am not lacking in creative imagination!

I had the last treatment of that initial chemotherapy in April 2002. My family surprised me by turning up later that day and accompanying me to a special Chinese restaurant that they knew I loved.

The joy of seeing them, and having time together, really marked the end of that season of treatment.

My consultant thought that I would be ready to climb Ben Nevis in the summer. Alan and I started to do a bit more walking together than we had previously done, and would drive to the Peak District for a half-day's walking, sometimes joined by Philip and Emma, who expressed a desire to climb Ben Nevis with us.

We were busy throughout the time of the treatment planning Charlotte and Austin's wedding, which was going to be on the 13th July, 2002. They also expressed a desire to climb with us. We set the date for some time during the week commencing 12th August as, by then, the newlyweds would be back from their honeymoon.

As my heart has been very much for the nations of Eastern Europe, we decided we would ask for sponsorship for the climb. The money would be used for the pioneering work of the ministry in Romania, Moldova, Belarus and the Ukraine.

The spring of 2002 was a fairly intense time: we were trying to build up my energy with regular exercise, planning the climb, organising a wedding and all as soon as the last treatment of chemotherapy was given.

It was the love of Jesus and it was so indescribably pure, accepting, deep and overwhelming.

Chapter Seven
Holding Steady

The lumps had responded well to the treatment. All had shrunk and disappeared from my body apart from marks where they had been. Then, in late June, just a couple of weeks before the wedding, I noticed a very small lump at the back of my scalp and one on the trunk of my body. It was a blow. I had to apply everything I had learnt to hold steady. Alan and I chose not to share this with anyone at the time because we didn't want anything to mar Charlotte and Austin's special day.

Straight after the wedding, I went for a further biopsy and, yes, the cancer was still there. It was a hard appointment to keep at the clinic.

I want to share with you something I discovered at this time. I kept seeing truths in the Bible that helped me so much. If you read the account of the baptism of Jesus, in Luke 3:22, God says,

"You are My beloved Son; in You I am well pleased."
Luke 3:22 (NKJV)

Turn over the page to Luke 4:3 and we read about Jesus being led by the Holy Spirit into the wilderness and Satan says, "IF you are the Son of God."

I saw this pattern: what God says, opposed by what Satan says. At times we will all have a choice between what God says and what the world says.

What had God said to me? You shall not die but live. I will heal you. What was I being told medically? The cancer hasn't gone; the treatment hasn't dealt with it. I had to dig deep, draw strength from that hidden source of life and choose to flourish and be fruitful.

The stitches from the biopsy site were due to be removed during the time that we had planned to be in Scotland to climb Ben Nevis. We arranged that I would go to the hospital in Fort William to have them removed before the climb.

Alan and I managed to slip away to the appointment without the children knowing. We wanted nothing to spoil the week we were having together, with our venture of climbing the mountain.

We had booked a log cabin big enough to accommodate us all and we watched the weather carefully to see which day would be the best. We agreed that Monday 12th August would be the day, so that morning we drove to the car park. At exactly 9am the six of us started the climb.

Nothing in the Peak District could have prepared me for what lay ahead. It is a five mile climb so in all 10 miles. Let me explain...

A ten-mile walk is quite a challenge but this is five miles up and five miles down. I was carrying excess weight due to steroids and I had only finished chemotherapy four months earlier. Looking back, it's nothing short of a miracle that I got to the top.

Once again, I learnt so much during that day. The children could have reached the top in a fraction of the time but they set their pace to mine. I was okay as long as I could see the summit but as we got higher, we lost sight of the summit and then I really struggled. At times the tears were rolling down my cheeks but I was so determined to do it.

Our son-in-law, Austin, noticed and he drew alongside me. I noted what he said: he asked me if I really wanted to get to the summit, to which I replied that I did. He said, "If you really want to keep going, then I will match my pace and walk alongside you. We will do this together."

Alan was so determined that I got to the summit first and so it was, that the six of us walked to the summit together.

As a leader, I have from time to time drawn alongside a potential leader, someone who I can see is struggling, and I have posed the same question to them as Austin did to me. We need encouragers, and to be encouragers, to enable others to fulfil their God given destiny. We need to be willing to get alongside one another, in order that each can achieve their destiny.

My claim to fame is that I probably hold the record for taking the longest time to climb up and down Ben Nevis. It was exactly 9pm and going dark when we got back to the car. Twelve hours! My knees had swollen with the pressure of the steep steps coming down the mountain and the next day I walked around Fort William extremely awkwardly...but we'd done it.

After the results of the biopsy were taken in the summer of 2002, it was very difficult as the lesions and lumps, which had originally been limited to my face and head, were spreading over the trunk of my body. My face was very sore with lesions and very red. I had a nasty lump on my stomach and a number of lumps on the bottom of my spine.

I had to hold on to the words that I surrounded myself with. In 2 Thessalonians 3:16 it says, "Now may the Lord of peace Himself give you peace always in every way."

I needed that and, I have to say, 99.9% of the time that is what I experienced and lived in. The 0.1% of the time was when I took my focus off the promises of God, and listened to the medical reports or what other people thought.

In the early autumn, my consultant advised me that he wanted me to see a lymphoma specialist at a neighbouring hospital for a second opinion. I found this appointment beyond hard.

He was very professional, direct and abrupt throughout the meeting. He examined me and then said that the chemotherapy hadn't dealt with the cancer. He also informed me that it was spreading. He talked at us rather than to us, but I cannot remember anything he said apart from suggesting that I would soon need palliative care. He drew on my notes where the lesions were located and there was a big angry one on my stomach. He left us for a while and went into an adjoining room. He must have been speaking into a recorder, as we could hear some of what he had said during the appointment.

What I do recall is that he referred to, "The husband being nonchalant," and it felt like I had been stabbed in my heart. I looked up the definition of the word nonchalant as soon as I got home. It means "casually unconcerned or indifferent". This amazing, steadfast, trusting, strong and faithful man was being totally misrepresented and completely misunderstood.

It's something that I have observed quite often since then: if you are peaceful in a difficult or serious situation, people think you don't care. I recognised it from when our parents were ill, dying or at their funerals. We were held in that perfect peace of God which can appear to others that you are hard or don't care.

The specialist gave us an appointment to go back on 5th November when he would pursue the provision of palliative care. I can assure you that over the following weeks we continued to pray for the lesions to go and on that morning of 5th November there wasn't one skin tumour visible. As we started the appointment, he asked me how I was and how much further had they spread. I said that they had gone but it was only when I was examined that he accepted what I was saying. There was no explanation for this and so he discharged me back to my consultant, which I was very happy with.

My consultant felt that he should closely monitor these comings and goings of the skin lesions over the trunk of my body, and not give any further treatment at that time. I believed this was the right thing to do.

Over the next three years, the lumps would come and go on different parts of my body — but always only on my trunk, below neck level and never on arms, legs or anywhere where they couldn't be covered by clothes. I never went swimming or exposed my skin to anyone other than Alan. I would always have at least one or two lesions, often more, and I got used to them coming up and then shrinking down. It became the norm. My face was very red, sore and disfigured.

I was still having regular appointments with my consultant at the hospital and always came away very cheerful. My consultant would suggest that I attend the clinic the following month, or three months, and jokingly ask if I could check my diary first to see if the appointment was convenient for me to fit in with my travel plans.

It was a private joke between us that he had to fit in his appointments to see me around my busy diary. He was very affirming, encouraging and thrilled that I was carrying on with my responsibilities throughout this period of several years.

We still had a mortgage at this point, not a massive one, but one that still had some years to run. We were advised that because the cancer was life-threatening we could, under the insurance cover, apply to have it paid off but we never even considered applying because we knew that it wasn't going to be life-taking for me. God had spoken that I would be healed so we couldn't have it both ways. Either we stood on the promise of God or we took advantage of what the world was offering. We couldn't do both.

Interestingly, it wasn't long before we were in a position to pay off our mortgage in full. I love God's ways!

In May 2003 (two years after the lymph gland biopsy and removal that had left me with constant pain and gave me difficulty in raising my left arm or turning my head) Alan and I were again on holiday in Scotland on the Ardnamurchan Peninsular. We had rented a cottage and spent most of the week either by the sea or in and around the cottage itself.

On the last day of our holiday, we had decided to go for a walk through a forest which, on the map, wasn't far from our cottage. After we had been following the map for a while, we became a little disorientated. The path that we thought we were following through the forest was actually taking us out of the forest and up the side of a mountain. We stopped to re-orientate ourselves. Whilst doing so, a man came down from the mountain and, as he passed by, he said that we had chosen a great day to climb to the summit as the views were fantastic. He said you could see all the different islands and highlands around. Now it had never been our intention to climb the mountain, but I have to say that this is a shared love of ours, and once the thought had been planted, then I really wanted to get to the summit.

It was a good challenge and it required us to take view breaks from time to time to catch our breath. On one of these view breaks we spotted the cottage we were staying in. As we climbed higher and higher we started to see such delights unfold, things around our cottage that we had been totally unaware of during the week of our stay.

Each increase in height brought new aspects. We saw a loch, streams and waterfalls that were all in the close proximity to the cottage that we hadn't been aware of before. It was only from above that we could see them. God spoke so powerfully to me through this. I started to share with Alan what God was showing me: how we can be so fixated on our immediate circumstances that we miss all the other good things going on.

The Bible tells us we are seated in heavenly places with Jesus, that we should see things from heaven's perspective and not be so earthly bound that we miss the heavenly; that we weren't created to peck the dust like chickens but were created to soar like the eagle.

Whilst I was enthusiastically sharing these revealed truths with Alan, I noticed that I could turn my head with no difficulty or pain. I was so excited. I lifted my weak and painful arm, and it was no longer weak or painful. I had been sovereignly healed by God.

When we set off up the mountain, I was in need of healing. Whilst on the mountain, I was healed. In one moment, I became able to move without pain. Following this, strength gradually developed and today I have full power and movement in my arm.

I had accepted that my appearance was not attractive to look at. My face was very sore, marked and red. I had a deep strength to draw on whenever I looked in a mirror. God continued to reveal to me my true identity which underpinned everything. There were a couple of occasions around this time, however, that really threw me.

One was when Charlotte asked if I would like to go with her to buy an outfit for her first interview after leaving university. Charlotte is a beautiful woman inside and out. When she had selected a number of items of clothing, in a well-known high-street store, we asked if we could go to the changing rooms for her to try them on. The member of staff looked me up and down and then blanked me completely. It was as if she couldn't accept that someone so beautiful as Charlotte had a mother who looked like I did. I managed to hold it together until Charlotte had made her purchase, and gone back home, before sobbing my heart out over this incident.

Another was at an event when someone I know through ministry made a personal reference to my appearance and my weight. I had to constantly remind myself of who I am in Jesus, how much He loves me, approves of me and exactly what He thinks about me.

I had many worship songs that helped me through these years but a song based on Psalm 62 and 71 was a wonderful assurance to me.

You are my Rock in times of trouble

You lift me up when I fall down

All through the storm

Your love is the anchor

My hope is in You alone.

One friendship that was growing was with Tina, the young woman from the North West. She was hungry for the things of God. I had been invited to speak at another event in North Yorkshire and was delighted to meet up with her again.

From that night, a deep friendship developed between Tina, Alan and I. It was a friendship we both knew we wanted to invest in. It was a great joy to get to know her family and later her boyfriend, who we quickly grew to love too. Alan and I were thrilled to be able to participate in their wedding in August 2005. They, and their children, have become a huge part of our lives.

Tina sums it up like this:

"Over a year after we initially met, I heard of Anne again, and that she'd been having cancer treatment. I felt inexplicably sorry that I hadn't been there for her. I went to hear her speak at another local meeting in which she told stories of amazing things that God had done during the treatment. For example, terrible bruising disappearing from her hands and arms, just in time to allow another dose of chemo.

"My heart was newly hungry for God, and Anne spoke of the Holy Spirit in ways I had not heard before. We talked after the meeting, and Anne prayed for me. Neither of us can remember how we went from there, to the first time I travelled to visit her! I know we had both felt a significant connection, and in a short space of time, a close friendship grew between us. It has been, and is, an honour to share life with her."

During 2002, and for a couple of years afterwards, there were a lot of issues that really tested my faith, my peace and my call, but plenty of positives too.

There were quite difficult times. Alan was very unhappy at work. He had been given a role within the company that meant he was away from home a lot. He was doing a job that didn't suit his personality and it caused him a great deal of stress. We missed the children now they were both married, living some distance away and busy with their own lives, churches and careers. I did struggle at times with the re-appearance of the tumours and all the ongoing hospital appointments.

In 2003 I went, with the other leaders of the ministry, to the USA for a conference. We were invited to afternoon tea, in the suite of the conference hotel, with the CEO of the ministry. She greeted each one of us by name as we went into the room.

When she greeted me, she looked right into my eyes and in that instant, I saw Jesus and I wanted to dissolve. The love that I saw has never left me. I saw His love for me. I don't know how I managed to hold it together. I had never seen such pure love. Of course I am loved by Alan, the children and so on, but this was very different. It was the love of Jesus and it was so indescribably pure, accepting, deep and overwhelming. I can still picture it today and it moves me when I recall it.

It was an important part of my story because I knew that, as the song says, "All through the storm Your love is the anchor. My hope is in You alone."

From the turbulent year of 2002, through to 2006 when I so needed to hold steady, His love was my anchor and my hope was in Him alone.

One of the prayers that we regularly pray is that which Jesus taught us in the Bible: the Lord's Prayer. We can say it so often that we can easily lose sight of what it is we are saying.

I like the following minimalisation of it: Father, Your will, Your way, Your provision, Your forgiveness, Your guidance, Your deliverance, Your glory. For EVER. I continued to focus on His way, His timing, His provision, His everything.

My focus constantly had to be to look at Jesus and see who God is. I had to constantly trust God for what He has done through Jesus. God is love and Jesus demonstrates this. He demonstrated this love through dying for me. His death was not the end and so, for me, death is not the end. I will one day die. We will all die but He has triumphed over death. It is all about Jesus and what He has done for us in love.

It is in Jesus we see how God has dealt with suffering and death. We see the purity of His love as we draw close to the risen Jesus. The implications of accepting and trusting this is that I have been reconciled to God, as opposed to being separated from Him.

I have a set of Russian dolls from when I first went to the Ukraine. One day, I was doing something with them when God showed me this simple truth. If I represent one of the middle-sized dolls, then when I accepted Jesus by faith as my Saviour, He took up residence inside me.

I placed a smaller sized doll inside the doll representing me. This internal doll represents the fullness of the Godhead, Father, Son and Holy Spirit. I then took a larger doll and placed the one representing me, also containing the one representing the Godhead, and placed it inside the larger doll which represents Jesus again. Now I was sandwiched, hemmed in, protected, covered and secured. I saw that I was hidden with Christ. This greatly affected my identity, my belonging and my security.

This simple illustration with the Russian dolls, demonstrated to me what I had partially previously understood. That my body is a temple of the Holy God. I have become holy, not because of my behaviour but because of my position. It is where God is, that is Holy. Therefore, it is His presence within that makes us holy.

Another thing I learnt during this time is that whatever Father God wants to communicate to us comes via the Holy Spirit. He simply shares with us what He hears shared in the throne room. So, whenever I got a sensing of a word from God, or prophetic and tested words given, it was the Holy Spirit telling me of things to come, that had been shared in the throne room.

All the sensing, and the revelations, that were accumulating in my spirit were being given by the Holy Spirit, listening in to what had already been agreed.

John 16:13 tells us that whatever He hears, He will speak and tell:

"However, when He the Spirit of Truth has come, He will guide you into all truth for He will not speak on His own authority, but whatever He hears He will speak and He will tell you things to come. He will glorify Me for He will take of what is Mine and declare it to you."

John 16:13 (NKJV)

That meant that it was already agreed in Heaven that I would be healed. The Holy Spirit had heard this in the throne room and I was open to receive, into my spirit, what He was sharing.

Throughout these years I was still ministering and travelling full-time, fitting everything in, in a way only God could do; family, church, community, home. There was a lot of upheaval, changes, difficulties and indeed they were turbulent times.

The positives were that Alan and I were closer than we had ever been. Both children were happily married and establishing their own Christian homes. They were growing in their faith and taking on responsibilities within their own churches. Eventually, Alan had the opportunity to have his old job back, within the company, which he was so happy about. I was seeing God move in my life, and the life of my family, in powerful ways.

It was becoming quite normal for me to go out speaking and preaching the Word. I'd pray with, and lay hands on people, see them healed, restored and yet know that under my clothing, there were a number of tumours on my skin. I reached a point of acceptance that this was how it was going to be.

I was invited to share on a number of Christian radio programmes and it was while I was speaking on air, in January 2005, that the interviewer asked me what I would like on my epitaph. I had the length of a song going out live before I needed to give my response.

I recalled the passage in Acts 13:36 where it says,

> "When David had served God's purpose in his own generation, he fell asleep."

Acts 13:36 (NIV)

When the track had finished playing, I replied with, "Anne, after she has served the purpose of God to her generation, fell asleep."

That has not changed at all. That is my heart: to serve the purpose of God to those around me. It was that same day that I had a strong sense of something being conceived inside me and God saying that because I was trusting Him, He would give evidence of gestation and expect a full-term delivery in September.

That September, I attended a conference in East Anglia where I was going to speak alongside other invited speakers. One of those was a woman of great faith and during her sermon she spoke about how easy it is to accept things rather than believe for the fulfilment of what God has promised. I got a real stirring that this was a word for me. I had become accepting of how the disease was in my body. It was sort of under control but still there. I asked her if she would pray with me about the lymphoma.

She said that I had tolerated the disease and it was time to stop! There was no messing with this clear word. What you tolerate you cannot change. I had not realised until re-reading my journal that this was going to be the full-term delivery that God had spoken into my spirit the previous January. I came away from that conference very uplifted, and yet there was no change with my skin.

In November 2005, just a couple of months later, I again flew to the international conference for the ministry and during one of the sessions our CEO spoke about how many of the leaders had received prophetic words that had yet to be fulfilled.

She encouraged us to consider if there were any outstanding words that we needed to stand on in faith. She then said that she believed there were leaders of nations who were waiting for the fulfilment of promises of healing.

I was up and out of my seat in a flash. This one was for me! Many stood in the large auditorium, but it was as if it was only me. I stood in faith and asked God to complete that which He had promised and to completely heal my body of all the tumours, lesions, cancer cells, everything. I was no longer going to accept the coming and going of the lumps was normal. I was asking for total healing.

The year ended with the wonderful news that Charlotte was pregnant. They had chosen to share it with us as soon as they knew because they wanted us to pray that everything would be alright with the baby.

Charlotte had been advised to inject medication daily throughout the pregnancy, in order to support carrying any baby to full-term. We kept this news to ourselves, as asked, but it gave us a joy and something precious to look forward to.

We were revelling in God's faithfulness to perform His promises and I believed, deep in my spirit, that 2006 was going to be the year of my healing from non-Hodgkin lymphoma.

He would split the sea and I would be able to walk through the waves to the other side.

Chapter Eight
The Unfolding

We started the New Year of 2006 with great joy: Charlotte had a hospital appointment on 17th January for a scan and the midwife confirmed that the baby was due on 3rd September. The baby was 12.32mm long and they could see head, arms, legs and the heart beating. The scan on the 14th February showed the outline of the baby with a little nose and eyes. The wonder of it all just caused us to celebrate God even more.

I asked Charlotte what I could do for her during her pregnancy and she said simply, "Pray for me and the baby." I assured her that I would. Then she asked specifically for prayer for when she went into labour.

I said that I would pray for her through the early stages of labour until it was time for her to go into the hospital. I reassured her by adding, "That's a promise. I will keep that time free in my diary for you."

I blocked out a large chunk of time in my diary so I could keep my word.

It was February 2006 when something on the news caught my attention. There had been a dreadful landslide in the Philippines and the reporter said that the problem was made worse because there were no tree roots to prevent the slide.

I thought of God's Word in Jeremiah 17:7-8:

"Blessed is the man who trusts in the Lord and whose hope is the Lord. For he shall be like a tree planted by the waters, which spreads out its roots by the river, and will not fear when heat comes; but its leaf will be green, and it will not be anxious in the year of drought, nor will it cease from yielding fruit."

Jeremiah 17:7-8 (NKJV)

I recognised that over a period of time, it was as if my faith had grown deep like the roots of a tree. As I had been searching out the things of God, I had been drawn close to the water source: the Holy Spirit. I suddenly realised that a gradual work had been taking place, much like the growth of a tree.

I have a cousin who took a seedling that had started to grow in her garden. She planted it in a pot and over a period of time kept transplanting this seedling in ever-increasing sized pots. Finally, the seedling could no longer be kept under her carport as it had grown so much. She had a friend who was the head gardener at a National Trust property and he took the tree and planted it within the grounds. Five years ago, Alan and I went with her to visit her tree. We took photos of her with it and could not believe how big it had grown. Recently, we returned to the grounds and, to our amazement, the tree was even more enormous. We compared the photo from five years ago with the photo taken this year, and we could see how much it had grown. This is what was happening with my faith.

It started with that first step of salvation in my teens and through life's circumstances it was as if I was being re-potted until, at this point, I was amazed at just how deep my roots of faith had gone. As it says in the aforementioned passage, despite the heat, despite the drought, despite external circumstances, the tree would retain its green leaves and would continue to be fruitful, and so it was with my life. This was another milestone moment for me.

The lack of roots on the trees in the Philippines had contributed to the landslide. But the deep roots of my faith were continuing to be established, and would hold me steady in any storm, challenge or giant that I had to face.

That Christmas, I started with what I diagnosed as the flu. It was a real attack on my body. I felt very poorly, weak and tired. I rested as much as I could but felt like I was struggling to get through each day physically.

The ministry was holding a four nations conference in Romania at the end of February, and I was not only going to be one of the speakers but I was also the organiser. I loved it but I felt really unwell. I had never recovered from what I thought was the flu. The conference went really well, but I was exhausted.

On the morning we were due to fly home, there had been a heavy snowfall which caused the airport to close. We had to find an alternative way home, which involved driving the length of Romania and then flying via another country. On the flight home, I asked my colleagues if I could have a two-week sabbatical to try and get over the flu.

I explained I had completely run out of energy and the incredible ability I normally had to push through. The Duracell Bunny's batteries were flat!

I was still on that sabbatical, and still unwell, when the March 2006 ministry conference in Southport came around. It was as much as I could do to sit upright, and I felt so unnaturally weary. In fact, I would lie down as much as I could during the conference. It was during one of the sessions that I received a word linked with the Exodus of the Children of Israel from Egypt. I recognised that God was telling me something I needed to take serious note of. The speaker said something along the lines of, "The Red Sea was ahead and the army of the enemy was rapidly approaching, but just when it seemed there was no way out, God opened up the sea and they were delivered."

I felt waves of revelation going through my mind. I knew this was a direct word from God. This was not the topic that the speaker was talking about; it was just a throwaway line within what they were actually addressing. I heard nothing more during that conference.

Let me explain the story: The Children of Israel had been held in slavery in Egypt and were being mistreated; but they were learning how to become a nation. God called a man, Moses, to go to the Pharoah and ask him if he would let God's people go so that they could move to another land. There they could be a nation who would demonstrate, to other nations, who God really is. Pharoah said a very clear 'no' despite being on the end of a number of very unpleasant plagues.

Eventually, Pharaoh reluctantly agreed to let them go, and so the Children of Israel moved out of Egypt and walked as far as the Red Sea. It would have been a massive move of people, animals and possessions. It would have taken some time. After they had gone on their way, Pharaoh had a change of mind and together with his army, went after them.

The people found themselves with the barrier of the Red Sea ahead of them and the army of the largest nation of the then known world chasing after them. They were trapped! Just before the army reached them, God split the sea open and the people were able to pass through to the other side. The army charged into the open passage, between the walls of waves, intending to get to the people and destroy them. God caused the waves to roll back on the pursuing army and they were totally wiped out. God's people were safe on the other side. He destroyed that which was trying to destroy the lives of His people.

What I heard was that things were going to look, and sound, like they could not get any worse, but just at the last minute God would make a way for my healing. He would split the sea and I would be able to walk through the waves to the other side.

I read and re-read that passage from Exodus 14:13:

> "Do not be afraid. Stand still and see the salvation of the Lord which He will accomplish for you today. For the Egyptians whom you see today you shall see again no more for ever."

And verses 27-28:

> *"So the Lord overthrew the Egyptians in the midst of the sea, then the waters returned and covered the chariots, the horsemen and all the army of Pharaoh that came into the sea after them. Not so much as one of them remained."*

Exodus 14:13, 27-28 (NKJV)

Please take time to read this chapter from Exodus 14. It was the explanation to me of what was going to happen.

I received this as a direct word of healing; that when things looked like they couldn't get worse, at the very last moment, God would open up a way for the cancer cells to be killed and not one would remain. My healing would be forever, and it was not going to come back.

I continued to prepare myself for the extensive time of heat that I sensed I was shown through Jeremiah 17. I tried to prepare myself for the time when it would appear nothing more could be done. I did this by enveloping myself in worship songs, reading the promises from the Bible, praying and resting.

I asked for an extension to my sabbatical from the ministry. I was so weak that it was as much as I could do to get up and take care of my own personal needs. I would lie and read, pray or just be for hours, day after day.

Another passage from the Bible that was given to me during this time was Psalm 20:7-8:

"Some trust in chariots, and some in horses; but we will remember the name of the Lord our God. They have bowed down and fallen; but we have risen and stand upright."

Psalm 20:7-8 (NKJV)

I received such a lot of strength and encouragement from these words. I was not trusting in the means of getting healed, I was trusting in my Healer. Strength and encouragement came to me from people from all over the UK, and further afield, who were communicating through cards, letters and emails. I knew that I was being prayed for, not just in the UK but in many other countries too. I knew that people were fasting and seeking God for us as a family.

I smile now as I recall that I was asking God for another scripture, a personal one that would be the Word that I would stand on. All I kept hearing was, "Total eradication." I felt certain that the word 'eradication' didn't appear in any of the versions of the Bible that I had access to, but I still searched. It was sometime later when I came to realise a truth. I was still standing on, believing and trusting the Word, and the manifestation of His presence that had occurred in May 2001. I would not die, but live and declare the works of the Lord. That the sickness would not lead to death, but was for the glory of God, and that Jesus would be glorified through it.

All the other words and Scriptures that were being given to me personally, and to us as a family, were all building on that word.

All affirmations of that word were pointing to the day when this disease would be totally eradicated from my body.

> *"Then the waters returned and covered the chariots, the horsemen, and ALL the army of Pharaoh that came into the sea after them. Not so much as one of them remained."*

Exodus 14:28 (NKJV)

God would make a way for me to walk through the sea which, for me, was the cancer!

My condition continued to deteriorate and I was unable to pick up my responsibilities within the ministry. The rest of the leadership team covered any speaking engagements I had, all the administration responsibilities and over-sighting. There was no pushing through this time. I was struggling to walk. I found it exhausting climbing the stairs. I could not manage housework so I spent most of my time in the garden under a gazebo, reading, sleeping, praying and just being. My breathing was laboured. I did not know at that time that I had quite a lot of fluid on my lungs.

Alan carefully filtered who should visit me, and I was so grateful. I only needed to hear the Word of God and not human opinion on how ill I was. We were so blessed with the friends we had, many of whom we had made through the ministry I was part of.

One of the couples who came to visit me was pastors John and Sandra, who always brought a word of encouragement and a word of life. We would share communion together. I had learnt the power of taking Holy Communion and would often do so with Alan, but more often on my own and sometimes more than once a day.

I felt there was such a power in this simple act of remembrance of all Jesus has done for me — for us. I felt that as I took the symbol of the bread, I was celebrating with gratitude what Jesus had achieved through His body which was broken for me. As it says in Isaiah 53:5:

> *"But He was wounded for our transgressions, He was bruised for our iniquities, the chastisement for our peace was upon Him and by His stripes we are healed."*

Isaiah 53:5 (NKJV)

When I took the symbol of the wine, I was celebrating with gratitude His blood freely spilt for the forgiveness of my sins, the remembrance of the covenant and me being a covenant child of God. I found this act very powerful, very intimate and extremely strengthening spiritually.

I cannot even begin to describe the difference between when I was unwell in 2001 and now in 2006. I felt that I was cocooned in God's presence and anyone who visited said that I positively glowed with His presence. I was so grateful to those who travelled to spend time with me. They brought affirmation, words of life and great peace.

I recorded in my journal on 21st March that one of the ministry leaders gave me the word about the woman being healed as she touched the hem of Jesus' garment. Then again, on 3rd April, another ministry leader gave me the exact same word. I typed up a few of the words I was given and I would carry the A4 paper with me and read and re-read until these words were deep in my spirit.

They were:

Matthew 8:13:

"Then Jesus said to the Centurion, 'Go your way; and as you have believed, so let it be done for you.' And his servant was healed that same hour."

Matthew 8:13 (NKJV)

And Mark 5:34:

"And He said to her, 'Daughter, your faith has made you well. Go in peace and be healed of your affliction.'"

Mark 5:34 (NKJV)

I learned through all of this, that His presence is sufficient for everything. I learnt what it is like to live moment by moment from His presence. Physically I continued to get worse. Alan and I both felt we needed a holiday and we had booked some days away in April (Easter) to go to Scotland.

I was seeing the GP weekly and he was doing blood tests and examinations, but just kept giving me another appointment for the next week and then the next week.

He said I should go on holiday but I was not well enough to pack, so my sister Ruth came over and did that for me.

Whilst there, I became more and more breathless. I was so unwell and hardly able to walk. One of my breasts became engorged and started to swell up.

As soon as I got home, I contacted the hospital and asked to speak to my consultant but he was away at that time.

They suggested I went up to the hospital to have a mammogram. In order for me to cover myself with clothes, Alan had to buy a size 22 top because of the swelling. I am usually a size 14!

When I presented myself for a mammogram, they couldn't do it because my breast was so swollen it would not fit in the machine and it hurt so much. The lady responsible for doing the mammogram seemed shocked by what she saw and asked me to wait outside the room while she went to speak to someone. A few minutes later, they called me in to see another consultant. He asked if I could go back the next day to have a core biopsy on my breast. In terms of pain, this procedure was off any scale. I just had to focus on God's love for me and His presence with me.

The reason why my breast was so swollen, and painful, was that there had become a blockage in the lymphatic system under my armpit.

It was a tumour that was causing the blockage and creating a type of lymphoedema of the breast. What I did not know was that my consultant was due back at work the next day. When he realised what was going on, he rang me at home and asked me to go in for treatment as an in-patient.

The following day, I was admitted to my local hospital and put in an isolation room. It happened so quickly that I could not let anyone know. At that time, you were not allowed a mobile phone in the hospital, so I was suddenly isolated from everyone.

The non-Hodgkin lymphoma had transformed to be more aggressive. The first thing that happened was they drained quite a lot of fluid off my lungs. That eased my breathing straight away. It was a procedure carried out in the room whilst Alan sat alongside — he was amazing. I was so poorly that I needed him to remind me of what God had said.

I was too poorly to read my Bible, pray or worship, but I had a little music player that had a few choruses on and I used to play that sometimes. I just lay and felt so encompassed in His presence that I did not need to say or do anything.

Another consultant came to visit me, in my room a day or so after being admitted, and asked how I was doing. I told him that I was 'fine now'...that's a term I used when I wasn't in extreme pain! He said, "I don't know about fine. Let's describe it like this; you were hanging over the ledge, clinging on to life by your fingernails, and now we've pulled you back a little towards the ledge."

It was a very hot day and he tried to open the window in my little isolation room, but he couldn't because of the limiter on the window which stops anyone throwing themselves out. I remember it so well as I was thinking I'm not going to do that; I'm here because I'm going to live, not because I want to die.

I saw my consultant who advised me that they were going to give me a strong course of chemotherapy over the next few weeks. This was to attack the aggressive cells and, hopefully, get them under control a bit, and then he would decide what to do next.

He said that I would need to go down to the operating theatre for surgery to insert a Hickman line into my chest. This would be the line they would use to administer the drugs directly into my body.

The next day, I was to be 'nil by mouth' ready for the surgery. The problem was that it was quite late in the day when I was to go down to the theatre and I sensed that my blood sugar was dropping. I recognised the symptoms from previous occasions when my blood sugar would drop and I would need to lie down and take something sweet to stop me shaking and fainting.

I recall a nurse coming into the room to check on me, and I explained to her how I was feeling. She said she would go and check with someone and left the room. I knew that time was important as I felt like I was going into a deep faint. Suddenly, into my mind, came the words of a song that I had learnt as a teenager at the 'barn rallies'. We used to sing some verses from Psalm 19:10.

The words were lifted straight from the Bible and set to a lively tune played on guitar, "Sweeter also than honey and the honeycomb."

I kept hearing over and over, "Sweeter also than honey and the honeycomb!" I thought, "That's exactly what I need at this moment in time – some honey."

My thoughts then went something along the lines of, "I need something sweet that honours the 'nil by mouth' so that I can have the surgery. I need honey."

Psalm 119 :103 (NKJV) says,

"How sweet are your words to my taste, sweeter than honey to my mouth."

Psalm 119:103 (NKJV)

I thought, I have the Word in me. Please Jesus, the Living Word, would you become like honey in my mouth? Before another thought came, I stopped shaking, the fainting sensation dispersed and I became steady again. This all happened in a matter of seconds.

When the nurse returned, which was sometime later, she found me smiling and steady. I was ready for surgery, much to her amazement and that of the nurse she'd brought with her. It was such a testimony!

I could hardly wait to share with Alan when he came to visit that evening. I was so excited as I knew it was a miracle. This is my God, my Jesus, my healer. No, the disease had not gone, but He had yet again touched me and made me well.

I had appropriated the written Word, through the Living Word and it had become a reality in my body.

As the chemotherapy treatment started a couple of notable things took place. I began to feel a little stronger, physically, so that meant I was a bit more on the offensive, spiritually. The other thing was that an ulcer had formed on the side of the engorged breast under my armpit which broke down and started to weep. This was not good in the environment I was in.

I started to be much more expressive about my condition and the fact that I was going to get better. This must have been a great concern to the staff because, medically, I was still compromised and the problem with the ulcer compounded that. I shared with any of the nursing staff or doctors that I needed to get well as I needed to be home before the beginning of September, when our first grandchild was going to be born.

They either smiled and said nothing, or smiled and expressed how unlikely that would be.

There were all sorts of dangers, such as infections, that were extremely serious in my situation as I had a suppressed immune system. I couldn't have flowers in my room, even though my mum and dad sent a bouquet to the hospital. They were kept in the main ward and I never saw them.

Anyone who came into the room needed to be gowned up and couldn't touch me. My bed linen had to be removed and placed into special containers because of the substances from the chemo that were being secreted out of my body through sweat.

Alan or Ruth took and brought back a freshly laundered towel every day from home. My sister spent many days sitting in my room when Alan was at work. If she wasn't in the room, she was at our home doing chores because I had been too weak to do any housework for weeks. She has the sweetest servant heart of anyone I have known. She is in the background causing no drama, no fuss, just doing it.

Charlotte was only allowed to visit once because of the unborn baby and the high doses of dangerous drugs that I was receiving. It was such a joy when she came and she left me smiling for ages afterwards. I suggested she went and got something to eat and then come back to my room.

When she came back, I asked her what she had eaten. She replied that she had chosen a very healthy salad but baby had chosen a cake. It was something that I still recall so clearly all these years later. Whenever I pass the food outlet at the hospital, this comes to mind.

Philip and Emma were excitedly preparing for a holiday to Canada, which had been a long dream of Philip's. I so wanted them to go ahead and I prayed that nothing happening back home would detract from their special time. They went but I was thrilled when they were back and eventually able to visit me.

Very few people were allowed to visit while I was in hospital but, to be honest, I felt too poorly to want to see them. Alan's workplace was so kind and gave him quite a lot of time off. They knew me well as I had worked there for many years and their kindness didn't go unnoticed.

Pastor John, who had visited me in the garden to share communion, came a number of times and we would share communion together. I was so peaceful apart from the occasional conversations with my consultant who mentioned stem transplantation. I knew so little about stem cell transplants and they say a little knowledge is a dangerous thing. All I had heard about was the harvesting of stem cells from aborted babies — I don't even know if that was true, but it caused me to be very unsettled.

It was on one of Pastor John's visits that I asked him to pray for me about the suggestion that I have a stem cell transplant. He was so knowledgeable; it was a subject he had looked into from a Christian/Biblical point of view. He said that he had done a study on it with his church and that there were certain conditions that he felt were acceptable alongside Scripture and our faith. It was so good to receive such practical help and advice because I did not know at that time just how important this was going to be in my story.

I appreciated the fact that he was up to date with the issues of the day and was able to talk through with me any concerns that were so relevant to my situation. His opinion was that providing the stem cells were from a known source, or my own body, it was a possible means of God healing someone.

There were tremendous highlights during those weeks of isolation. The cleaner used to come and, depending on how strong I was, I would engage in conversations with her. One day, she said something about my husband walking through the ward and I queried how she knew Alan was my husband.

She said that he was a man with a shining face just like mine shone. I was astounded! So often we don't realise what people see in us without us needing to speak.

Every time he visited me, just before he left, Alan would anoint me with oil. It meant such a lot to us both. I noticed that the nurses would stand to one side if they were attending to me to allow us to share that quick but precious moment.

In 2005, while at a conference in the USA, I had purchased some body lotion. It had a fresh scent and each day I would rub my legs with this lotion. The body lotion was linked, in my thinking, to the promise that I was reminded of: that God was about to fulfil His promise made years ago.

The nurses told me that they just loved to come into my room as it smelt nice. I always smiled and expressed appreciation for whatever they were doing.

I don't fully understand it, but the best way I can describe what I was sensing is that I felt God had allowed me to be there for that period of time, simply to be, simply as a vessel of His presence in that place.

Another really precious thing was that our friend, Tina, sent me a postcard through the post to the ward every single day that I was in hospital. Each card was a photo from a beautiful weekend Alan and I had enjoyed the summer before with Charlotte, Austin, Philip and Emma. Tina had helped me organise digital photos some time prior to me being admitted to hospital. She wrote an encouraging verse of scripture on the reverse of each card. These daily blessings were such a delight.

They brought my family close, visually, reminding me of a fun weekend of joyous relationships, which helped me focus on doing this again in the future.

I found that apart from short periods of worship, or during the day if either Ruth or Pastor John came, I had so much time on my own. I knew that I needed to keep my mind fixed on the promises of God and I had a few practical focuses that I kept going over in my head.

One was to be home to fulfil my promise to Charlotte, that I would pray with her during the early part of her delivery, the other was to make some changes at home to our bathroom.

I felt that if I focused on something that involved the future, I wouldn't allow the thoughts of death to swamp me. I did think a bit about dying, about my funeral service and about the impact that my death would have on my loved ones. I wasn't afraid at all, but I did so want to live. I wanted to have years of companionship with Alan and to grow old together.

I wanted to be an influence within the family, on my future grandchildren and I wanted to do the things that had been spoken over me prophetically which I felt, as yet, I hadn't fulfilled.

I have to include this, because if I didn't it would not be sharing the full story. Whilst I had thoughts about dying, they were not from the aspect of fear but from knowing that for me to live is to portray Christ to a desperate world; to die would be my gain.

On days I felt strong enough, I drew up plans in my head for the revamped bathroom we needed at home, and found inspiration from watching a couple of daytime television programmes which featured restoring property.

This was also the year of the football World Cup and, when Alan left me at 8pm, I would tune in and watch the football which made the evenings shorter.

I learnt through some of the staff that a bug had hit the ward and everyone was contracting it. This was potentially serious with the suppressed immune system I had. I lay in my bed and commanded the bug that was rampant outside my isolation room not to come over the doorstep. I later learnt I was the only person on the ward not to get it.

Was God going to, yet again, show Himself, His plans, His intentionality, His purpose, His nature in this timing of the transplant?

Chapter Nine
The Fulfilment

The issue of the possibility of me having a stem cell transplant was gaining momentum. My consultant shared that he had spoken with someone at a large teaching and pioneering hospital and they had expressed an interest in my case.

He was thinking of sending me to meet a doctor at Queen Elizabeth Hospital, Birmingham, to talk through the possibility of me having this treatment. The doctor was also a Consultant Haematologist, just like my consultant, and she was based at the regional centre in Birmingham with an interest in using stem cell transplantation to treat blood cancers.

My consultant asked if I had any siblings. I shared about Ruth and Michael and he said the hospital would contact them to find out if they would be willing to be tested for compatibility with me. Needless to say, both Michael and Ruth came to the hospital for testing.

Whilst I was still an in-patient at Stafford Hospital, my consultant said it would be necessary for me to go for an appointment to meet with the doctor in Birmingham. I asked if I could go by car, with Alan driving, rather than be transported by ambulance.

We met with the consultant and I remember feeling so weak and weary that it was as much as I could do to take in all she was saying.

During the consultation, she referred to the fact that the cancer was at stage 4b, which was the first time I had heard this applied to my condition.

She was so lovely, professional and caring with us. She outlined what the procedure entailed which was that the stem cells would be taken from one of my siblings, if they were compatible with me, and transferred to my body after receiving a mega-blast of chemotherapy. Alternatively, the stem cells could be harvested from my own body and then returned back to me, after the intense course of drugs.

We asked her what she thought would be the best way forward and she said we had limited options because without this stem cell treatment I would soon die. From a non-medical point of view, I came away from that consultation with this understanding: without the stem cell treatment I would soon die.

With the stem cell treatment, using stem cells harvested from one of my siblings, I would have a one in four chance of it working, but a one in five chance of my body rejecting their stem cells and dying. If I had my own stem cells harvested, I stood a much greater chance of surviving the transplant. However, there was a high risk of the cancer being reintroduced back into my body, if there were lymphoma cells in those cells harvested from me.

I recall all these odds, lots of numbers and statistics which were all very important to hear, but I was thinking, "Wow! This is what it must have felt like to be one of the Children of Israel as they were trapped between the Egyptian Army and the Red Sea."

The odds didn't look or sound good. I needed some affirmation from God whether I should go with the stem cell transplant, and preferably with cells harvested from my own body. This whole treatment was a massive procedure and not one to be undertaken lightly.

We headed back to the car and as we were travelling along the M6 northwards, right by junction nine, I had this amazing wave of complete peace sweep over me, along with the realisation that whilst all that we had heard was a shock, none of it was a surprise to God.

Instantly, I knew deep inside that neither of my siblings would be compatible. I knew that when God formed me in my mother's womb He had known of this then. I knew that it was my stem cells that were going to be used, and that not one cancer cell would be reintroduced to my body once I had received the megablast treatment.

I shared this with Alan and I remember looking upwards at the gantry of junction nine and saying, "Alan, this isn't a problem to God. He's known from the beginning. It's going to be my stem cells that they use. It's going to be okay."

I was later informed that neither Ruth nor Michael were compatible so the plan was to go ahead with the harvest, and use my stem cells. I was very happy with this. By the middle of July the ulcer on the side of my breast had healed and the skin was like a new baby's.

Over the weeks of being an in-patient, I had needed to have regular blood transfusions, injections to prevent blood clots and lots of other interventions.

Now I was going to have a course of injections that would stimulate my body, to sort of 'kick' the stem cells out of my bone marrow into my blood.

The timings were important. At a planned date, when the medics believed the stem cells were ready, I would go to the Queen Elizabeth Hospital in Birmingham and have them harvested from my blood.

I don't have the exact dates because I had stopped journaling during this protracted time in hospital, but some days later it was arranged that I was to go again to Birmingham and have the stem cells harvested. Once again, I asked if Alan could take me in our car. After being out of 'normal' life for so long, these car journeys gave me some sense of the normality which I craved.

On arrival, we were taken into a room with a lot of equipment in it. There were two or three medics with us and Alan was allowed to stay throughout. I lay on the bed and was connected by cannulas to tubes which took my blood out of one arm, through some equipment and then back into my other arm. The equipment was called a cell separator machine and it worked by 'hoovering' the stem cells out of my blood and then storing them in ice. The procedure took several hours.

When it was completed, I had to lie and rest as my blood pressure was incredibly low. Alan then drove me back to Stafford Hospital.

As I was wheeled through the main ward to the isolation room, the staff started to clap and cheer. I was very moved but didn't understand why they were so expressive.

It was a little while later, that one of the senior nurses came and told us that the harvest had been amazingly successful.

The harvest they needed was equal to a formula number of three, and my consultant had warned me that if they didn't harvest sufficient stem cells the first time, they could repeat it twice more, but then that would be it. The staff at the Queen Elizabeth had rung ahead to Stafford, while we were on our return journey, to inform them that they had successfully harvested the number equivalent of 134. It was an outstanding harvest at the first attempt.

That was the day I knew I was experiencing God, my Deliverer. My lavish, abundant Heavenly Father was going to show His approval, His part in this. His hallmark was all over this harvest. To His Glory!

Occasionally, I was allowed to visit home for a couple of hours during the day. It was so good to be back in my familiar surroundings. I was only able to rest, nothing else, but it gave me the opportunity to have brief telephone calls with family and loved ones.

We rang both couples — Philip and Emma and Charlotte and Austin — and asked them if they would like us to share with them some of the details from our visits to Birmingham, such as some of the statistics that had been shared with us. Both couples declined as they only wanted to hear what God was saying, and not have their minds and thoughts filled with what dangers, problems or giants we might be facing. We accepted that, but decided we couldn't share with anyone else exactly how critical the next few weeks were going to be if we didn't share it with our children.

We decided to only share, in confidence, what the situation was with the leaders of the ministry I served with. Their support, and the love behind that support, was beyond words. Afterwards, I learnt that one precious co-leader had written my name on a piece of paper, and pushed it into the Wailing Wall in Jerusalem earlier in the year. It was an act of faith, believing for total healing.

Years later we returned together to Jerusalem, and joyfully placed another piece of paper into the wall, giving thanks for my healing. It's only symbolic but very powerful.

On occasional days at home, one of the other national leaders would come to see me, travelling miles across the UK to do so. Alan and I so appreciated their love and support. These were always days of being recharged spiritually.

It was the end of July 2006, when my consultant told me that he was going to send me home to wait to be called by the Queen Elizabeth Hospital for the transplant. Alan and I had received a wedding invitation from one of my nieces which we had, under the circumstances, declined. However, this wedding was important to me because when my niece was a teenager our relationship had been very close.

I not only had the joy of leading my niece through to salvation but also to the baptism of the Holy Spirit. I love this young woman deeply, as I do my other five nieces, and saw I had been given a window of opportunity to share in this special day.

Within a short time of being allowed home, looking much the worse for wear, I managed to spend the day with family and friends celebrating my niece's wedding.

Austin, our son-in-law, had the task of buying me a hat, I think it was as close to the wedding as the day before. No one else had time, and he made a great choice. I was again without hair, eyebrows or eyelashes, with marked and sore skin on my face, but I looked glorious as we celebrated God's goodness. It was so special to sing worship songs, corporately, as part of the ceremony. I was very aware of the presence of God at that wedding. Photos show a very radiant me and a very pregnant Charlotte.

As part of our preparation to go in for the stem cell transplant, Alan and I felt we needed to share with people the need for prayer. This was to cover us as they did the procedure. I asked the international ministry, where I served, if they could prepare a statement, which would be emailed throughout the members, to inform people what was happening. We were so grateful for this massive prayer cover.

Just one week later, I took a phone call on the Saturday morning of 5th August, 2006 from the Queen Elizabeth Hospital to say that a bed had become available and could I admit myself that afternoon. It was a shock as I had expected to go in on the Monday, but we quickly packed a few things and Alan drove me to Birmingham.

Timing now was interesting. I still believed, and was telling people, that I was going to be home before our first grandchild was born. I think no-one apart from me believed it.

I knew that the megablast of cytotoxic drugs would be spread over six days which would take us to 13th August. The stem cells would be transplanted back into my body the next day. I would then need a further two or three weeks in hospital which, potentially, would take us into the week commencing 4th September and baby was due on 3rd September.

Being called in two days earlier excited me, as I thought things would get underway quickly, and make my discharge earlier. However, the treatment didn't start straight away and was, in fact, started and ended as planned.

The chemotherapy treatment I was given was so strong, that without the transplant of stem cells, my body could not have recovered. During this intense treatment I was weak beyond words and it took every ounce of strength to shower, dry myself and get back into bed, but I persisted as this was the only time I used my voice to worship. A nursing assistant would accompany me, then leave me to shower and with the noise of the water in the cubicle, I would sing praise and worship, often in tongues, for the whole time. It became so important to me during these days that even when I felt too weak I would still attempt a shower. It was my only activity for the day. The staff were amazing and, once again, I received the highest standard of care and attention.

I was aware these were hard days for Alan. He is not one to show emotion in anyone's company, but he has written a short account of how he felt during these times:

"When Anne first received the diagnosis in 2001 it was a shock. When it was explained to us about the treatment, we both realised it would be a hard path to walk. I felt I had to keep any emotions in check, as Anne had always seen me as steady, never showing high or low emotions.

"Although God spoke to Anne, one night, and things took on a different perspective, for me it was not an easy path to walk. We did hold on to what God had spoken. We believed His Word and I also constantly reminded Anne of unfulfilled prophetic words over her life. I reminded her that she just needed to get better to fulfil them. I felt the responsibility of reminding her and assuring her. Many times I would hold her in my arms and she would say, 'Make me better Al.' There was nothing I could do except pray and hide the emotion that was inside me, as I knew it would not help her if she saw me fall apart. I wanted to be strong for her.

"We both love Scotland and it is our go-to place for a restful break. I remember going on holiday at one point in her illness, and standing looking out over the sandy beach at Gairloch Bay. Anne started to cry. When I asked her what was wrong, she said that she was wondering if we would ever see it again, together. It was hard to stay strong but my strength was from God.

"Eventually, Anne went to the Queen Elizabeth Hospital in Birmingham for the stem cell transplant and, although the statistics were scary, we still held on to the words God had spoken to Anne that night.

It was hard to leave her in hospital and drive home to a dark and empty house. Those were the times my emotions would spill out, and I would share them with God. I knew that the next day, when I returned to hospital, I would be greeted with a smile that would lift my spirits."

My birthday is 15th August. As that day got nearer, I felt stirred in my spirit. You see, when we had spoken initially with the doctor at the Queen Elizabeth, she had explained that the day you receive your transplant is the day you are 'born again'. You have a new start, you have a new birth day.

I smiled because I have already been 'born again' but not by the will of man, or by the will of the flesh, but born of God through Jesus. As the doctor explained, I would have a new birth day, I did just wonder.

I mentioned in Chapter One that in my childhood I perceived sadness around my birthday. Alan and I, over the years, had always tried to make that day special. Was God going to, yet again, show Himself, His plans, His intentionality, His purpose, His nature in this timing of the transplant?

The staff, at the hospital, had said that I was going to have the transplant on the 14th and then they changed their minds. They decided they needed to allow my body one day of rest at the end of the megablast of chemotherapy.

As the date got nearer, they confirmed that the date of my transplant would be the 15th August, 2006. This was a significant day.

I was going to have my new 'birth day' on my birthday! He knew my days before I was formed in my mother's womb.

I love what I see of the nature of God, in these small but important details. This has transformed how we celebrate my birthday; we don't need to try and make it special anymore — God has done it.

It was at this point that I shared that my actual birthday was the day that I was going to have the stem cell transplant. I don't know who was more excited, me or the staff!

Alan arrived early that morning and brought balloons and streamers, and decorated my bed. The procedure started, and medical staff never left me because of the seriousness of what was happening. I had noticed Alan carrying two plastic bags full of something. As he sat alongside, during the procedure, he explained that on his return home the night before, he had struggled to get the front door open. Behind the door were piles of envelopes with cards. Every card was a birthday greeting, which took me several days to open as there were 132 of them! Many of them contained an encouraging word to lift my spirit.

By the end of the day the transplant had been successfully carried out. I felt loved and full of joy. Alan departed with both of us so thankful, and peaceful, for what had unfolded that day.

I have hazy memories of the next few days. I remember a feeling of drifting quite a lot. I had a strange experience which made me laugh out loud, apparently.

It was as if I was bouncing on a cotton wool cloud, having such fun I didn't want it to end. I find words to describe these experiences difficult.

It was as if God was the cotton wool cloud and I was bouncing around with Him, in Him and on Him. It was fabulous! This was an aspect of God I had never been aware of before. God created fun and I can enjoy the purity of fun.

Throughout the days I was monitored very closely. I received a number of blood transfusions but remember very little else. I remember my brother, Michael, and his wife, Vicki, visiting and we talked about property in Spain as if nothing unusual was happening, but after they had gone, I returned to the feeling of drifting.

I remember Philip and Emma visiting and I was able to get out of bed and walk to the ward lounge with them, but I don't remember any detail. I remember just 'hanging in' and trying not to drift away completely.

One day, about a week after the transplant, I was asked to go to another department. I was expecting to be taken in a wheelchair, but a member of staff suggested I walked there. I remember only taking a few steps down the corridor and the floor coming up to greet me. I just sat on a nearby chair until someone came along, and then wheeled me back to bed. I think that was about the Tuesday or Wednesday.

A day or two later, on 24th August, just nine days after the transplant, the medical team gathered at the bottom of my bed as part of their rounds, and discussed me. There seemed to be some mix-up about my blood results.

The outcome was that I was to have the same tests done again, later in the day.

The next day, the same team gathered, but this time with the consultant I was under. It took me some time to grasp what they were saying. The previous day, when they had looked at the blood results, they were so good they had presumed that there had been a mix-up, which was why they had arranged for them to be done again. Here they were again — remarkable blood test results!

They said that on paper, based on all the tests they had done, I was fit and well enough to go home. It was the only time I panicked. I could believe that the results were excellent, there were so many people praying, but my physical body needed to catch up with those results. The thought of even leaving the ward overwhelmed me, as I was so weary.

It was the Friday at the start of the August Bank Holiday, and so the thought of Alan driving to Birmingham, picking me up and us driving all the way home, was too much for my emotions. I asked them if I could delay that until the next morning. I asked if someone could contact Alan and suggest that he didn't come and visit that evening, but instead he could come and pick me up the next morning. This was agreed on the understanding that I returned to the Queen Elizabeth Hospital on the Bank Holiday Monday for repeat blood tests, and to have the Hickman line taken out as I would no longer need it.

Alan was as shocked as I was, but he shared with the children what was going to happen.

He came and picked me up on the Saturday morning, and when we got home we were greeted by Philip, Emma, Charlotte and Austin. Charlotte was blooming. They waited on me all day long.

I lay on the sofa and just revelled in their conversations, banter and the joy of us all being together once more.

Charlotte shared how she wanted us to lay hands on her before going into labour. I couldn't but, to my delight, I lay on the sofa and watched as her dad, husband and brother all laid hands on her, prayed for her and the safe delivery of the unborn baby. It is forever etched in my mind. What a blessing.

Alan took me back to the Queen Elizabeth for 11am on the Monday morning. I went to my room and they came and took the necessary bloods and told us to go away for a couple of hours and come back for the results. We only went to the bathroom superstore nearby. I tried to be interested in what we were planning to do to our bathroom once I was better, but all I wanted to do was lie down.

When we returned to the hospital, I was so pleased to lie on my bed. The results had come back and they were even better than the previous Friday. They said they would take out the Hickman line and then I could go home. What the doctor hadn't realised was that Stafford Hospital had a method of inserting the line, deep into the body, under full anaesthetic, whereas Birmingham only inserted it under the surface of the chest.

She made an incision in my chest and started to tug and wriggle this line around.

After a reasonable amount of time, and my gritting of teeth, she gave up, suggesting it was removed back at Stafford. I could go home with the incision in my chest stitched up, but with the Hickman line still in. I was asked to attend the clinic at the Queen Elizabeth on the Wednesday, which was two days later.

Alan took me to the clinic and we again saw the lovely lady consultant who had only good and kind things to say to us. She said that everything had gone so well that she was happy to discharge me back to my consultant at Stafford. She also thanked us both for bringing something special onto the ward. She said that she had received many comments from the staff to say what a delight it had been to have me there.

I share this, because the delight doesn't come from me. I was simply hosting the presence of God, and He is the delight to be around. I couldn't speak more highly of the care I received from all the staff there. She discharged me from Birmingham that day, Wednesday, 30th August, 2006. I was able to be at home, apart from needing to attend clinic at Stafford each day for blood tests, have the Hickman line cleaned and to be examined.

I rested, spoke to loved ones on the phone and waited to hear from Charlotte to say she had started her labour. On Sunday 3rd September, just four days after being discharged home, we got the call: Charlotte was in labour. I fulfilled my promise to pray with her and our beloved granddaughter, Grace, was born at 11.36pm.

A couple of days later, I saw my consultant and couldn't wait to share with him, and all the wonderful nursing staff there, that Grace had been born and I was home to fulfil my promise. He suggested to Alan that he should drive me to Nottingham immediately to see the baby.

We have pictures of me holding her in my arms at just two days old. I look so frail and weak but, I can tell you, inside I was a roaring lion.

The next day I started to feel unwell. Alan was at work and came home briefly at lunchtime to check on me. I shared with him that I was unwell. When he got home in the evening, I said that I needed medical attention. I knew my body and I knew all was not well. In the end, Alan drove me to A&E. The doctor on duty listened intently to what I shared with him and he said that I probably knew better than him. He arranged for me to be admitted and put immediately onto intravenous antibiotics. That action probably saved my life.

The next day, when my consultant heard what happened, he visited me on the ward and had me transferred to an isolation room for continued monitoring and treatment. It was suspected that the cause of the infection was the Hickman line, but there were no theatres free for the surgery needed to remove it. The matter was so urgent, that a doctor performed the removal under local anaesthetic, whilst I lay on my bed in the isolation room.

It was Alan I felt sorry for because I couldn't help the sounds that came out of my mouth during the procedure. I rated different procedures on a scale of one to ten during these years, and this one was way off the scale!

I was soon discharged from hospital with regular attendances at my consultant's clinics. I had a scan on the 23rd October, 2006 which showed a reduction in the lymph nodes to 11mm (close to normal). I had a couple of follow-up scans: one in 2007 and one in 2008 and both showed there was no residual disease in my body.

I wrote in my diary, after the October 2006 scan, a verse from Joshua 21:45:

> *"Not a word failed of any good thing which the Lord had spoken to the house of Israel. All came to pass."*
>
> **Joshua 21:45 (NKJV)**

God will ensure that there will be a fulfilment of what He has declared. God is watching to perform His Word. He is intentional.

I continued to have yearly consultations until 2016, when ten years had passed, and then I was discharged completely.

Every single promise God made, every word spoken, was fulfilled in its entirety. Those eight months of 2006, from the January when I had flu-like symptoms, until the removal of the Hickman line, did, in fact, feel like I was between the Egyptian army and the Red Sea. But God did split the sea and enabled me to come through. Not one cancer cell remained. The disease was totally eradicated.

It's a story to be shared, not because I think it is, but because God says it is to be shared around the nations, for His Glory.

On 15th August, 2007, I wrote in my journal, "One year ago today I had the stem cells. I feel so very well it's hard to link the two things. It seems unreal now. Going for scan this week."

21st August, 2007, "Scan all clear. What God has said has been. Not one thing left undone. Thank you, Lord."

He has created us to soar like the eagle on the wind of the thermals of His Spirit, seeing things from a heavenly perspective.

Chapter Ten
Soaring Like the Eagle

I have had so many people say to me, "You need to write a book." I knew that sometime this was exactly what God wanted me to do, but it needed to be His time, not mine. I would smile as prophetic word after prophetic word would come to me about writing the book. I even called it 'The Book' as I gathered things together that, one day, I knew would be used in its writing.

In Exodus 9:16, God addresses Pharaoh, through Moses, and explains that He (God) is going to use the whole situation to display His power and that His name will be declared throughout the earth. I believe that this has been God's intention through the story of my healing.

Through the writing of this book, and wherever I have verbally shared this or part of this story, God's power is displayed, and He is being glorified throughout the nations of the world. This is how intentional God is. As I have written, I have seen the details of the weaving together, the circumstances that have built in and through my everyday life, that show a transformed life. A life that would have read very differently without it being surrendered to God.

I have had to overcome all sorts of obstacles whilst writing. Going back through the whole story of the original diagnosis, the prognosis and multiple medical procedures brought everything flooding back. As I typed the script, I would sometimes become exhausted.

I always spent time in prayer and worship before I started, and I typed under the anointing of God, believing that this is a book that will bring glory to God. Whilst, hopefully, it is an interesting story, I trust that it will be a teaching tool for many too. Over the years, people have spoken over me that I have a special teaching gift. This gift is not only for the spoken teaching but discipleship through everyday life and activities. That is why the book incorporates stories, because I know that God can speak powerfully through them.

Whilst in the midst of writing, I started to feel nausea and a discomfort in one of my breasts. Initially, it was hard to identify the discomfort, but within a couple of days it was clearly my breast, and it was clearly becoming more tender. My GP examined me and confirmed that I had not one lump but two – one pea sized and one much larger.

He fast-tracked me to the breast clinic and I knew the enormity of this; however, it was so noticeable how I responded. I hadn't heard anything from God about this situation and, after a couple of days, I expressed this to Him. Later, as I worked in the kitchen listening to a familiar worship song, I sensed God saying that He hadn't said anything because He didn't need to reassure me this time. I sensed Him saying, "You know that I have this. You don't need Me to tell you what I know you know."

I had only shared the situation with the immediate family and I received from them, later that day, a couple of pictures and promises from God. The discomfort continued and it was joined by a dragging sensation from my neck and armpit area. It was a sensation that I well recall from before.

In the mirror I could see that I looked poorly, and also on Zoom I could see the pallor of my face. I simply kept praising, sleeping and focusing on the things of God. I chose to share the situation with a close group of praying friends.

A week later, I was part of a Zoom meeting with a team from the UK and Uganda. An issue came up in our sharing that caused something to rise within my spirit. I started to speak into this and shared a couple of verses from the Bible. Then, I began declaring who God is and who He is in our circumstances. I then prayed into all this. As I did, I sensed something shift deep within me.

After the Zoom, I went to Alan and said, "I think something significant has just happened to me."

The letter came from the hospital, and the appointment was a couple of weeks further away than I had expected the fast-track appointment to be. I said to one of my ministry partners that this was because it was giving time for my healing to manifest. That is exactly what happened. By the time I had the appointment, both lumps had gone and I was discharged with the all clear. The only thing was, I still had this dreadful dragging sensation from my neck and armpit.

The day after discharge, Charlotte rang to tell me about something she was dealing with. During the conversation, she mentioned something about how complex our minds are. As soon as we had finished the call, I addressed my mind in the name of Jesus, and commanded it to align with the truth of God's Word, the truth of my healing and for this sensation to stop.

I got on with whatever I was doing and, hours later, I suddenly noticed that the dragging discomfort had gone!

We are in a constant need of being alert to the tricks and lies of our spiritual enemy, which manifest and appear to be real, but we have the weapons of warfare and can stand in the power of Jesus. We do have an enemy, the one whose kingdom we were transferred from at the point of our salvation. He fears the glory that God intends for our lives. He knows that if we come to a place of understanding, of all that God has done for us through Jesus, we won't be held back by doubt or fear. I have noticed a pattern over the years in that health issues seem to be where the enemy attacks me, but I have a greater power at work in me, and His name is Jesus.

My friend Tina sums it up like this:

"In the years since her cancer treatment, Anne has told me — usually several days afterward — about various accidents and health-related incidents. One day she had become so breathless at the hairdressers that they called an ambulance, despite her protests. I somehow didn't associate that with her having survived a pulmonary embolism years earlier. Then, at some point, she told me of a scary night-time episode and paramedic attendance. While they waited for the ambulance, Anne experienced a sensation of something moving in her chest when Alan prayed for her. Her breathing returned to normal but blood tests and scans confirmed multiple clots in her lungs for which she was put on long-term anticoagulant therapy. I've lost count of the bumps she has taken since, with barely a bruise.

"When, much more recently, Anne asked for a phone call despite having plans to meet soon, I had a sense of foreboding. Anne's cheery voice reassured me that she was in a good place, but what followed was a story of sudden pain, a GP visit and referral to a breast clinic because of a significant mass. I listened and assured her of our prayers. Coming off the call, I remember feeling such dismay. 'God, what is this about? I don't want to lose my precious friend.'

"It was good to spend time together, just a few days later, before the scheduled investigations. As we talked, she acknowledged the enormity of what might well be ahead, but we shared total peace. It's hard to explain, but as I'd prayed since the phone conversation, I'd found myself with a deep and clear conviction. Anne won't be dying until God is good and ready to take her. Her experience has actively confirmed this over and over.

"Far from an arbitrary 'name it and claim it' approach, we hold onto what God has specifically made clear and, in the absence of that, to the practiced knowledge of His faithfulness. They went to the clinic, I prayed all morning and checked my phone repeatedly. At 11:22, a message from Anne had such wonderful news. 'Whatever it was has gone! They've done various scans and ALL CLEAR. On our way to have coffee and a scone...full of praise and thanks for God's healing power (again).'"

As I prepared to write, I knew that it would centre on how God revealed His love to me. How He called and equipped me and how, whatever I do, I do in obedience through His leading and direction. Discovering my true identity has been a major part of this.

We are God's idea, created in the image of God Himself: Father, Son and Holy Spirit. He always wanted to have a people on earth who would share His life, nature, Spirit and purpose. That is what all the ups and downs, the good times and the struggles work towards in my life.

As I have studied various passages in the Bible over the last few years, I have learnt that we can know Jesus's victorious fullness as we walk through the challenges of life. We do not need to be subject to our circumstances when we have the fullness of the Godhead within. God has designed each one of us to be, both personally and corporately, as the church. He wants us to be ministers of the fullness of Jesus, everywhere we go. We minister as a living body, demonstrating His wisdom, portraying the beauty, peace and glory of Jesus. He has ordained that we should go from glory to glory, growing and maturing in faith. He has created us to soar like the eagle on the wind of the thermals of His Spirit, seeing things from a heavenly perspective.

It is not enough, to give mental assent to the statement that God loves me. John 3:16 says, "God so loved the world that He gave His only begotten Son that whoever believes in Him should not perish but have everlasting life."

This love is the agape, unconditional love of God, in order that we should not perish. The word perish here describes the loss of well-being. God's intention for you, and me, is that we should not lose our well-being, but instead have life in all its fullness. We need to receive the love of God, deep into our hearts and very being. Romans 5:5 says,

"Now hope does not disappoint because the love of God has been poured out into our hearts by the Holy Spirit who was given to us."

Romans 5:5 (NKJV)

In the letter to the Ephesians 3:17-19, the writer prays that we might be so rooted, and grounded, in love that we can know and experience the reality of the love of Jesus Christ, which surpasses intellectual knowledge. This is so we might have the richest measure of the divine presence in our lives, and become a body filled and flooded with God Himself.

This truth has become so clear to me over the years, especially the years of the illness. As a teenager I knew and believed that 'God so loved the world', and I gave my mental assent to that but it took the challenges of life for me to grasp the depth of that love, the reality of that love and the impact of that love that has shaped me into the woman I am today. I was, and am, transformed by His love.

Much of our life, and the relationships we develop, flow out of who we believe we are, what we perceive our value to be, and where we see our life going. So many events in our lives, particularly in our youth, can distort and devalue who we perceive ourselves to be.

We who have committed our lives by faith to Jesus carry the very DNA of God. We are carriers of His presence.

In 2 Corinthians 4:7 it states that,

"We have this treasure in earthen vessels, that the excellence of the power may be of God and not of us."

2 Corinthians 4:7 (NKJV)

What that means, is that we are like fragile clay pots containing the dynamic presence of Almighty God. We are His testimony on earth, called to demonstrate not just His love but also His power. We need to understand, then align with His will, and then His glory and power will spill out of our lives, portraying who Jesus is. God wants to be able to use us to carry out His plan in the world. You may think that you are limited to an insignificant location but, wherever we are, God has positioned us, so that we can demonstrate His glory.

What I have learnt is that His life, His presence, His resources, His power, His wisdom and His love live within me right now. The day I received Jesus by faith, I received the ability to walk as He walks, think as He thinks and live as He lives — but I didn't know that.

I believe a key to understanding, and activating this truth, is found in John chapter 15, where Jesus talks about Him being the vine and us being the branches. It's the vine that contains the life. The sap flows through the vine to the branches. This illustrates our connection to Jesus. Even though we are joined to Him (since our salvation), He still tells us to abide in the vine. That means we must, through a deliberate intentional act of our will, consciously draw on the sap of the life of God within us.

We do this through deliberately developing our relationship with Him, such as time spent in intimate times of worship, offering statements of love, gratitude and honour. We need to prioritise, in our busy lives, times of simply revelling in His presence and listening to Him. We need time where we can focus on Him, the work of the cross, the empty tomb and the Majesty of the Risen Christ.

He has done everything to save us, but when it comes to transformation, we have a part to play! That is to hold nothing back from Him, to surrender our lives in obedience out of devotion. We will see the power and life of the Holy Spirit break out, and transform every area of our lives. We were intended for relational connection with the living God. That is why He designed our hearts to run on fresh encounters with Him, and fresh revelations from Him. In the same way, our natural relationships cease to function well if they are not consistently invested in. They need investment of time as well.

God wants us to be confident in Him and in His love for us. As well as being Almighty God, He is deeply personal and intimate. He enjoys relationship with us and wants us to enjoy our relationship with Him. God does not want religion! He is looking to have a relationship with each one of us.

God is the All Sufficient One. We do not need to live our lives from a place of lack or need, but from a heart that has been healed and restored by receiving and embracing His love. Our spiritual enemy still tries to tell us the same old lie, that we are inadequate.

Then, we try to make up the perceived deficit by focusing on our fears, failures and inability. But the Good News is that we have a new identity as children of God.

We are seated in heavenly places with Christ Jesus. We are new creations. The old has gone and the new has come. We have become His covenant children through the broken body and shed blood of Jesus. We are recipients of His grace, His love, His mercy, His righteousness, His glory, His Kingdom, His name's sake.

It is such an amazing truth that as we respond to Jesus, we see ourselves as God sees us and we are free to be who we are destined to be. It is so important for us to understand that God is not a killjoy.

I want to share how important it is for you to look again at how you see God. You see, we are shaped by the image we carry of Him, and this determines how we live and the choices we make.

A whole new facet of God was revealed to me while I was recovering from the stem cell transplant. I shared with you how I felt. I was bouncing in Him, on Him, through Him while recalling the laughter, the fun and the freedom. It was something new to me. It was a revelation! The boundaries God places on our lives are not something to spoil enjoyment, it is quite the opposite: it is so that we are safe within those boundaries, to have that enjoyment and freedom.

A spiritual shift started in me in the spring of 2017 when I began to feel that I was no longer where God wanted me to be.

I did not want to make a decision that was not in obedience to God. I had a stirring on the inside that wouldn't go away.

Then, in the summer, during an enforced time out of ministry, I recognised this feeling was not going away. We had been told that my father only had a few days to live, so as a family we were sitting at his bedside during his final days on earth. This gave me the gift of a lot of quiet time to reflect, ponder, pray and also celebrate. Within a short time, I knew that it was time to lay down my leadership role in the ministry, and simply wait on God for whatever lay ahead.

It was strange because I believed I had a life call to that ministry, and I had interpreted that as continuing in leadership. I rapidly realised that a call to a ministry isn't necessarily in a leadership role. I acknowledged, that by aligning with, praying, supporting financially and generally encouraging the ministry, I was continuing the life call. I will always be indebted to the leadership of the ministry for all that I learnt during the years, and for the trust they placed in me.

In obedience to God, I stepped down from leadership, and on the day I did, God spoke into my spirit that I was 'to be' and not 'do' for the next twelve months. Any concerns that I would feel isolated after working as part of a team for decades, were replaced by the most wonderful sense of presence. A presence, that at times, has been overwhelming and I have never felt isolated.

I felt as if I could fly, and this feeling has continued. I know that I am doing exactly what I was called to do.

I am walking in my unique identity, in alignment with the call of God on my life. It is the most liberating place to be and my spirit is soaring!

The four months after laying down the leadership role seemed to pass very quickly, and then Alan and I went to Scotland for a holiday in February 2018. We were in a little cottage in the Cairngorms when the 'Beast from the East' arrived and dumped several feet of snow, literally on the area we were staying in. We were trapped and couldn't get out to get home. Towards the end of this time, we were walking in the snowstorm and, in my head, was having a conversation with God. It went something like, "Okay, God! You said about 'being not doing' but I'm not sure if I'm doing it right. I'm not sure if there is anything I should be doing."

Without realising, I started to speak these thoughts out loud and so started to share with Alan what I was feeling. He, as ever, listened intently but said little. It was just good to share it with him.

After a snowplough had managed to get through, the road was open to single lane traffic. The local farmer scraped the drifts of snow off the drive and we dug our car out and we set off for home. It was very late when we arrived, so I didn't check emails or messages until the next morning. When I did, I was stunned to have received an invitation to pray about being part of an apostolic mission to the nation of Peru.

Peru! My heart skipped a beat. In order for me to explain, let me take you back to my childhood. I had enjoyed primary school; it was a small village school based on relationships and family friendships.

It was a great place for learning and our headmaster was someone who imparted his passion to the pupils.

One topic that completely enthralled me was about Peru and the Inca people. I would have been about eight years old and I remember so clearly becoming very concerned over their spiritual situation. I was concerned that they worshipped the sun god, and not the One True God who was revealed through the written Word (The Bible) and the Living Word (Jesus). They had no opportunity to learn about either. I think I drove my parents crazy asking what would happen to those people. It wasn't their fault they didn't have a Bible or know Jesus. I carried this passion in my heart, from my childhood, and shared it with Alan. Apart from my parents, siblings and Alan, no-one else knew about this.

To receive this invitation was incredible. I knew instantly that this was of God and that the answer was to be, "Yes!" Exactly one year to the very weekend of stepping down from the ministry, I found myself on a plane, bound for Peru. Once again, this shows the faithfulness and intricate detail of God to His word.

Prior to going, I received some very encouraging and unexpected communications from a number of people. They shared that they believed God would show me what was to be the next season of my life, while I was away in Peru. I received a message from a friend who said, "God is getting ready to open doors to new territory," and that, "You need to be ready for new opportunities. Don't look back; there's no returning."

On the 20th July 2018 I received a word, via another friend, who quoted Isaiah 55:5:

"Nations who do not know you shall run to you because of the Lord your God."

Isaiah 55:5 (NKJV)

Just before leaving for Peru on 30th September, 2018, I received the following powerful words from a prayer support friend: "This is the day you must run with Me. I have drawn you to My side and won your heart over and over again, but today I call you to run with Me. There are lives you will touch, and many changes will come, because of the light of My Son within you so run...run with Me, where I take you, even to the high places where you've not been before. Run! Be ready at all times to be My voice to the nations and My light to the world. Now is the time. You will run with Me into your destiny and calling. You have said to me, 'I will go and be who You have called me to be.' This is the season where your destiny becomes clear. Don't be afraid of what comes, for what comes to you, will be more of Me, my child."

While I was in Peru ministering to others, God was speaking so clearly to me. I am so grateful to have shared the whole experience with a precious friend who witnessed everything unfolding. Val was alongside me as the prophesies were given, as the mandates were given, as words were spoken over me. Even as we turned to the Bible in our rest times in our bedroom, God was making a number of things extremely clear. I felt it was an assignment for the rest of my life.

During these days in Peru, God gave me a number of mandates. I use the term 'mandate' because they weren't negotiable. God clearly asked me to do certain things, and one of those things was to write this book. It was clearly His timing. Writing a book has been spoken over me many times over the past three decades, but this time God said, "NOW is the time."

In January 2018, I met with three prayer support friends. During our time together, the ministry, which I have called 'Created to Soar Ministries with Anne Donaldson' was born. I believe it was inspired through the Holy Spirit as I have felt, for the past number of years, that I am soaring like an eagle.

I believe one of the calls on my life is to encourage others to soar into their God-given purpose. I am celebrating what God has done, and continues to do, in and through my life. I thank Him that I know His purpose for my life. I live in the fullness of Jesus and that I experience the love, joy and peace that only He can give. I thank Him that I know who I am in Him. That He has set me free from fear, from lack of purpose and that my identity is secure in Him. I thank Him that He has given me revelation and wisdom to deal with issues in life, and that I carry His presence with me wherever I go.

Just after the ministry was established, I stepped outside one morning and noticed something very significant. I had been given a clematis plant by my parents for a birthday present and it had successfully lived and flowered for 15 years in the same pot.

In the autumn of 2018, however, just before going to Peru, I cut the plant back to its roots as it had become pot bound and needed a transplant. I had forgotten about it over winter, and this particular morning I gasped as I saw all the new growth springing up. It looked like a different plant.

I sensed the Holy Spirit say that when He had given me the mandates in Peru, it was like He was cutting me back to my roots and that, suddenly, a whole new structure was coming forth.

Since then, it has been my privilege to minister to people in nations across the continents of the world. I know that He is fulfilling the word he gave me back in January 1996, when He showed me first the UK, then Europe, then South America, then Africa, then India and then the rest of the world. God is at work fulfilling His word to His Glory, "That you will be a witness to the ends of the earth."

The truth is, that having surrendered my life to God, I have found life in all its fullness. I am loving it! I have had the boxes ticked in a way only God could tick them. I am experiencing the adventures, the stretching, and the challenges that invigorate me. I would not change a thing. I am totally passionate about the person of Jesus Christ and all that He has done for me. I am not ashamed of the gospel. It is the power to save, the power to heal, the power to set free. Yes, I get very excited about Jesus. I am so blessed and I want to say publicly, "Thank you Jesus, for who You are and all You have done for me."

ANNE DONALDSON

About the Author

For relaxation, Anne Donaldson enjoys baking, watercolour painting, and exploring the beautiful countryside around her home in the Staffordshire Moorlands. She and her husband Alan share a particular appreciation for walking in Scotland.

Anne's love of people spills out into everyday life. She delights in building relationships to see others grow and mature in their faith. She loves nothing more than to be with her family, including for fun, fishing, or multi-season barbecues, as well as being there for one another in the difficult times.

Anne treasures her Christian heritage, and her faith has been underpinned by this. Her own experience of God's transforming love fuels her heart for others. Experienced in leadership, and with a recognised gift for teaching, she remains in awe of opportunities to worship, teach and minister around the world. Anne's passion is to see diverse people-groups finding their true identity in Jesus, and experiencing life in all its fullness.

ANNE DONALDSON

Created to Soar
M I N I S T R I E S
with Anne Donaldson

Following a prophetic word, Created to Soar Ministries was formed early in 2019. Created to Soar facilitates connections between Anne's ongoing ministry, local churches, prayerful supporters and opportunities to partner with others across the world.

In representing Created to Soar, Anne works alongside other leaders, joining them in shared vision for God's kingdom. Anne travels and speaks at Christian conferences and events in the UK and overseas. Through multiple unique expressions, Created to Soar helps to equip the church through promoting Biblical understanding, building up leaders and investing in humanitarian projects.

www.createdtosoar.com

Printed in Great Britain
by Amazon

78711874R00129